A CAT
IS WATCHING

A Cat
Is Watching

A Look at the Way Cats See Us

ROGER A. CARAS

SOUVENIR PRESS

SOME OTHER BOOKS BY ROGER CARAS

A Celebration of Cats
A Celebration of Dogs
The Roger Caras Treasury of Great Cat Stories
The Roger Caras Treasury of Great Dog Stories
The Roger Caras Pet Book
Harper's Illustrated Handbook of Cats
Harper's Illustrated Handbook of Dogs
The Custer Wolf
Monarch of Deadman Bay
Panther!
Sockeye
Source of the Thunder
The Endless Migration
The Forest
Mara Simba
Sarang
Dangerous to Man
North American Mammals
Last Chance of Earth
Venomous Animals of the World
Animals in Their Places

Copyright © 1989 by Roger A. Caras
First British Edition published 1990 by Souvenir Press Ltd.,
43 Great Russell Street, London WC1B 3PA

Reprinted 1991 (twice).

ISBN 0 285 62989 1

Printed and bound in Great Britain by
WBC Ltd, Bridgend, Mid Glamorgan

ACKNOWLEDGEMENTS

There really is no way to work back through a lifetime of experiences and friendships and single out the people who made all manner of things possible. At best you can spot-check, and that isn't very rewarding for anyone. I have learned about cats from a hundred people and probably from as many cats. I am grateful to all of them, human and feline, friends all. To my wife Jill, obviously, who gets to live and relive it all, I am grateful, but that isn't half of it. There is more than gratitude in thirty-five years of marriage! There has to be. To our kids, Pamela and Clay, and their chosen, Joe and Sheila, I am grateful for the sharing that made the best of it better. For my associate and friend George Dwyer, who read the manuscript and was never shy about making suggestions, I am grateful. For my cat-loving friends, among them Charlie and Jane, Roone, Rick and Priscilla, Joan and Howard, Paul, Cleveland and Marion, Sue, and another Sue, Christine, Ann, Bob, Meg and Sy, Eleanor, Joanna and Carlo, Shirley, Helena, Dick, Selena and Jesse, Sara, Tee, Amanda, Bob and Jean, Alan, Pat and Ed, Anne and Emily, George and Jorge, Mr. Robert E. Lull, Ian and Frank, Edith and Liz, Ditty, Bill and Galvin, Marie and Jimmy, Bess, Denise, Maybelle, and scores more, I am grateful for experiences shared and tales related. It is a special club, isn't it!

I think that it is to the cats' credit that neither Hitler nor Napoleon nor Alexander of Macedonia could belong. They feared and hated cats. It is not recorded that a cat ever loved any of that lot, either. But it is to the cats themselves I am most indebted. The most important lessons and greatest frustrations came from them. Let them all be aware, I am watching them, too. In that one way we humans have it all over our cats. We are the only ones who can kiss and tell. Since the things they can do vocally are not decipherable by us, the cat is in effect mute, and that is why this book has been written.

This book is for Sarah who is already a cat lover, for Joshua who is studying to be one, and to their respective parents, who set the stage; also for two young people eagerly awaited and soon to be here who will follow suit.
And for Marshall.

PREFACE

Before we begin our journey to what we hope might be the threshold of another kind of mind, we should have a premise. Actually such a premise is a collection of axioms, or *givens*, as they are often called today. They will not only guide us but will justify our exertions. There should be a reason for our going to where we want to go.

AXIOM 1: As humans we communicate with each other in more ways than we probably realise. Our voices and deliberate hand signals are only a small part of it. Posture tells us a great deal even when we do not consciously evaluate what is going on around us. Odour is terribly important, particularly because it heightens the acuity of our other senses and raises expectations. It also acts as a repellent and can be an alienator. Think of a crowded lift on a steamy summer day. Eye-to-eye contact can be of enormous importance and even inadvertent touch can be electric. Calculated physical contact can approach the ecstatic and surpass it if marked by acceptance and reciprocation. All of this transcends the spoken or written word and gesture by design. It is when we fail to identify the source of a signal or set of signals that we get all silly about ghosts and ghoulies and things that thrash around generally after dark. But we are tuned, even when we are not conscious of it, to another array of signals and by those signals act in ways we can't explain—we fall in love, feel elated or depressed, and certainly those signals govern our wanting to keep company with the likes of a cat. Often we communicate indirectly by doing or failing to do things people expect of us, or by doing the unexpected: showing up late for a dinner party or urinating on the kitchen table. Man and cat each have active ways of communicating that do not involve what we normally refer to as language. When someone is always late, always breathless with excuses, they are telling their victims about something far more significant than traffic jams. Freud said if you regularly lose your house keys you are communicating something else. You are not happy in your home and don't really want to go back to it. Communication is a very complicated matter.

AXIOM 2: Cats, as with perhaps all animals and certainly the so-called higher animals, also communicate with more than *mew* and *grrr* and *hissss*. We are no more certain of the many ways they have of sharing their lives and warning and advising each other than we are of our own catalogue of sensations and behaviour. We know they do it, we know we do it, but we are apparently still far from being able to put that kind of information together in a meaningful way. We know our cats, pretty much as we know ourselves and our fellow humans, as those fragments that are easiest to see. It is what I call shardism, this method of inferring information generally from fragments, although that is not yet an English word as far as I know. Shardistic knowledge is not really satisfying emotionally or intellectually.

AXIOM 3: Cats are cognitive. We don't even have a suggestion of criteria that we could use to measure how they think or what they think or whether thinking is a sometimes thing which they can turn on and off. More on that subject later. Cats are also by nature very stubborn and may resist what they learn and already know when it interferes with their essential character as voluptuaries. One suspects that if knowledge (which certainly must mean one thing to us and something quite different to cats) interferes with gratification, knowledge will almost certainly lose out. Cats often get into trouble because of this flaw in their nature. It brings them into harm's way. There is another thing we don't know for certain although we often think we do: are some cats more cognitive than others? Do they actually think more or just more often or just about different things? Are there smart cats and feline village idiots? Another mystery: is thinking enhanced or increased by necessity? We often hear that some cats are street-smart or perhaps, better, alley-wise. Do alley cats or feral cats in the woods and on the farm think more than our sofa cushions or just think about different things? Do we, when we gratify a cat's obvious desire to be the ultimate hedonistic materialist, deprive it of the need for cognition and therefore of cognition itself? We cannot answer that question, for our own cognitive powers fall short of the task.

AXIOM 4: Everyone who owns a cat is a cat watcher.

AXIOM 5: All cats, given the opportunity, are people watchers.

AXIOM 6: Since we have worshipped them, burned them, and hanged them as witches and worse, since some of us love them, some of us hate them, and not just a few of us are terrified of them, Axiom 5 is of some consequence. And since even the most seemingly gregarious among us are really very private (we show only what is on the outside, what we want others to see, and generally what we hope they will be willing to admire), it matters a great deal that a mysterious, cognitive creature is watching and perhaps understanding us in a way we cannot comprehend. It matters very much, I think, that in the lives of many of us *a cat is watching!*

1

quid shows in the course of a single day just about all of the traits this book is about. She is worth studying. She is our son's cat, really, but Clay and his wife Sheila and infant son Joshua went to live on Guam for a couple of years and Squid would have had to spend months in quarantine if she were to be sent out to them. A cage in a quarantine station is not her style. Being behind bars in a steel cage for all to see at their pleasure rather than hers would rob her of mystery, and Squid loves a mystery. That is particularly true if she creates it herself. She has a discernible sense of humour. If she has been here before, or if she is destined to come again, it was or will surely be as a creator of detective stories. She is the Rex Stout of the feline world.

Like all of Clay's cats (he always had at least two through college and medical school and through his internship as well), Squid is a "save." She is a Siamese that has apparently gone all wrong. She clearly descends from a blue point and something else. The blue-point part shows in her colour and the placement of her markings, but the splotchiness is one part of her little mystery. In fact, one of the fascinating things about cats is the absolute impossibility of ever deciphering that which we do not already know about them for certain. Some time ago, we can never be sure exactly when, two cats met somewhere around Boston. It was probably not a planned encounter but we can't be sure of that either and we will never know even approximately where it occurred. *Around Boston* is a big place. One of the trysters was at least part Siamese but we can never be more precise than that. There was a resulting litter. The number of kittens, unknown. The fate of any others, impossible to determine. All we have is silent Squid, who looks somewhat like a blue-point Siamese, and we can't even ask her if she had other owners before Clay and she met, or how they might have treated her. Surely there had to be someone because Squid was socialised when Clay discovered her in her hour of need. But she makes a game of it, of her relationship with people, and we don't know if that is a lingering effect of early mistreatment or whether that is her perverse sense of humour. I suspect the latter. I can't believe she isn't laughing at us.

Squid, for all her play acting, is a lover. She often does such intense figure eights around our ankles it becomes all but impossible to walk and that not just when she wants food, either. She seeks intimate contact because she apparently needs it. She appears from nowhere when you are trying to read or watch television and jumps into your lap or climbs up onto your shoulders to drape herself to sleep there. You wake up and find out that she has been sharing your pillow. No doubt about it, Squid seeks human companionship obviously because she craves it. She knows exactly how to get it and precisely how to maximise its pleasures.

But try to call Squid, even at mealtime. She has vanished. Without fail she is gone, has got out, dematerialised. No amount of coaxing will make her reveal herself in anything but her own good time, but after nearly a year and a half I have discovered her secret. Squid loves to watch people, especially when they are making fools of themselves looking for her. One moment she is under a couch with the frill of the loose cover draped across her forehead like the cowl of a medieval nun's habit. The next minute, chameleonlike, she has made herself integral with a piece of clothing or a pile of needlepoint cushions, but her pale purple eyes are always fixed on the person or people who are tearing the house apart trying to find her. She seems to dissolve or at least transport herself from one vantage point to another by momentarily surrendering her corporeal form. I have learned how to watch Squid watching us, by anticipating what her options are.

A cat knows how to anticipate. If they didn't, they could never hunt birds or mice or other sportingly fleet prey. They can anticipate and perhaps plot a prey's trajectory just as a golden or Labrador retriever can plot the arc and descent of a tennis ball or Frisbee, but a cat can't understand the concept of anticipation and therefore is unable to allow for it in other species. So this is where we have them almost surely. Cats virtually always underestimate human intelligence just as we, perhaps, underestimate theirs.

It is obviously fun to watch people scurrying about looking into and under things. We always open the same cupboards and closets to see if she has been locked inside one of them. We look under the same furniture as she dissolves ahead of us from place to place. We make silly squeaking *kitty-kitty-kitty* sounds which she clearly hears and apparently takes some considerable pleasure in ignoring. But she watches. Surely she has determined that the Squid-search ritual has a pattern and perhaps it is amusing for a cat to watch and call the next shot correctly. Eventually she tires of what is almost certainly a game. Then she materialises and strides across the room in full view. At which time everyone goes about their business recovered from the momentary panic Squid deliberately triggered. On those few occasions when she has in fact slipped by an arriving or departing visitor and got out, she has joined our indoor-outdoor cats for as long as it pleased her to be so associated, and then found a good lie of ground cover or a nice heavy bush and waited to watch people look for her in the garden. We amuse her in some way, inside or out. She has the talent of the cat to disappear and reappear at will and she uses her talents to insert a little play interlude into her otherwise fairly quiet day. The important thing is that people watching is a recreation that Squid not only enjoys but sets up at her own pleasure; she manipulates her surroundings and us. It is little different from our crossing the room and turning on television. What is it she is seeing when she is watching us? We will come to that.

There was another cat I recall that is worth mentioning. He or perhaps she (it did have a very broad face and looked like a big old tom, but one can never be sure) was a Texas critter of no apparent genetic affiliation of distinction, without so much as a clue as to possible lineage. He (for so we shall call him) was the kind of animal you would look at and say, "Thy name is cat."

A few friends and I were offered the use of a cabin on the edge of a stand of pecan trees about an hour's drive from San Antonio, near a town called Seguin. We were teenagers learning to live with the fact that we had recently become members of an elite club known as the United States Army and we had been given our first weekend off since being inducted. On our pay then, back in the forties, hotel rooms, even shared, were out of the question. After dreary weeks in the barracks the thought of a cabin in what approximated a wilderness for city kids, for such three of the four of us were, seemed like a gift created just for us on some higher plane. The

cabin's owner, an uncharacteristically kindhearted sergeant, told us we could expect a visitor. He had raised a great horned owl from the fluffball stage to adulthood and had then turned it loose to make its own owl's way between the trees of the night. But whenever the fierce hunter saw a light in the cabin, whenever the little building's windows glowed yellow, the owl knew it was occupied and came for a handout. We hoped it would happen when we were there, of course, but were more than just startled by that first violent tap on the glass in the window over the sink. There it was, great eyes peering in, body and head bobbing and swaying, the bird's whole demeanour demanding what it had been taught was its birthright. As we had been instructed to do, we put some meat scraps out on the lid of a box that held firewood near the cabin's only door and watched with enormous satisfaction as the mighty tyrant of the night flopped over from the sill and stared at us defiantly before settling down to eat. After a few minutes we went back inside and thought little more of the window over the sink.

I don't remember who saw the apparition first, but after about five minutes one of my companions muttered something about "here he is again." I looked over at the window and did a classic double take. It wasn't the owl at all; it was a fat-faced, dark cat, and it was sitting there watching us as if we were a scene from a movie. We got some more of the scraps we had saved and went outside again to lure this newest visitor to the wood box. Unlike the owl, a wonderful wild creature, the cat dissolved as soon as we stepped out of the door. We left the offering on the box and indeed it was gone in the morning. There was no way of knowing if the cat ate it, the owl on a second pass through the area, or some other woodland creature. There were a great many about.

Finally, about ten minutes after we locked the cabin door for the last time that night, the cat was back. When we moved, its head moved. Its eyes were always on one of us. It seemed to be more than just casually watching us: it seemed to be studying us or checking up on us in some way. Our every movement was a matter of intense interest or perhaps even concern.

We were up early the next morning—that had become a habit in the Army and fishing was on the schedule. The ultimately unrealised plan was to catch some fish and cook them for breakfast. When we went out, the cat was sitting on a stump about twenty feet away, watching the cabin door. I took one step in its direction and it disappeared, apparently into the nearby brush. People watching can be a great deal easier than cat watching. We don't yet have the power to dematerialise while cats clearly do. Fans of "Star Trek" can faintly hear them say, "Beam me up, Scotty."

We talked about the owl and the pussycat, for so we had come to think of them, several times that day. We wondered if the owl's season in captivity had taught it to accommodate its hunting instincts to allow anything as potentially tasty as a cat to live within its range. Normally a great horned owl would take a cat as exposed as our mysterious friend allowed himself to be. Even a good scrappy tom would not be able to defend himself from the talons of such a bird descending silently from above and behind and closing around its prey's spinal column. The flight of an owl is without sound because of special buffeting feathers on its wings' leading edges. An owl's night vision is superior even to a cat's. The cat does not travel with its claws pointed upward but an owl's talons are always pointed down. It would be a very unfair contest. We even worried a little about them, but the owl and the cat seemed to have come to some form of accommodation.

The most famous dematerialiser-the Cheshire Cat from Alice's Adventures in Wonderland, *drawn by Sir John Tenniel*

We spent three nights in that cabin that first time and some weeks later another two nights and the sequence was exactly the same. Shortly after we had finished eating there would be a startling tap at the window over the sink, rather like something Edgar Allan Poe might have invented for the occasion, and there the owl would be bobbing his strange little *me-me-me* dance and daring us to ignore the lord of the night sky. We would go out on schedule and present our offering and watch the bird feed, and then it would be gone, consumed by the night that seemed a living thing prowling between the trees. Five or six minutes (on one occasion less than three) after the cabin door closed, our second visitor would arrive. We put his offering out but never discovered whether he actually fed or not. He sat there just watching, on all five nights, at least until we went to bed. Once, after the lights had been out for about ten minutes, I switched on my flashlight. Mousebreath, as we had named him (it seemed original and amusing forty odd years ago) was not there. But he was always there on that stump, as still as a tomb stone, when we came out in the morning. We never heard him make a sound. We never succeeded in getting anywhere near him although we stopped trying after the second day.

Clearly that cat of the forest, a truly feral animal, knew a great deal more about us than we were likely to learn about him. One thing he surely could not have known: we would have liked to like him and would have been nice to him, had him in the cabin, fed him, petted him, given him a warm, soft place to sleep if he had come his halfway. Perhaps he didn't care. Judging from his size and condition he needed nothing we had to offer except ourselves as entertainment. He never made a mad dash to the food we put out for him, if indeed he ever approached it at all. But as long as the lights were on in the cabin he seemed compelled to watch us, turning his head, watching our movements and our non-movements alike. He was just plain people watching.

To this day I can't imagine how the fascination survived more than that first sitting, that first night. Watching a small cluster of human beings read or listen to a radio (no television in those days) must have been about as exciting as watching asparagus grow. But the cat did come back four more times after that first night to watch—not to interact, not, apparently, to ask for anything, just to watch. At least the mighty owl demanded and received food. What was it the cat saw in us? He wasn't manipulative the way Squid is today. He took us as he found us and apparently found more than a little fascination in that. We may be funnier than we realise. Or perhaps we generate vibes that excite cats or arouse something in them we haven't worked out yet.

People watching by cats is not necessarily a solitary affair. It can be directed towards a promising human activity pattern and can be done in concert. Several years ago we were invaded by mice. I don't mean those sordid, nondescript little things that presumably come off ships and in packing crates from other continents but field mice, enchanting white-footed, white-bellied wild little creatures that have been native to our fields and woodlands forever. They are creatures Beatrix Potter would understand very well (indeed, she did know all about their English counterparts, whom she described as industrious and tidy), but still they do eat the insulation off electrical wires which can lead to catastrophe, and they do leave unpleasant artefacts in the silverware drawer and cause you to create a trail of Special K across the kitchen floor when you set about getting your breakfast. I like these busy, bulgy-eyed, and graceful little creatures, but of mice and men together I do not sing.

Our invasion had to be curtailed, whatever our feelings about the invaders as individuals. In crowds they are destructive and obnoxious and they can be very expensive indeed. I checked the alternatives ancient and modern science had put at our disposal. The sticky baited cardboard tunnels that draw mice inside and fatally trap them by miring their feet in a tarlike glue were out of the question. They offer a slow and undeserved kind of death. They should be taken off the market. When we become civilised, they will be. The ancient technology of the cheese-baited snap traps that variously break the mouse's back or neck while fast enough to be apparently painless seemed inexcusably short on aesthetics. Every creature has the right to try to survive. Poison was clearly out—bad for mice and bad for pets, of which we have a great many. The most promising answer seemed to be a wind-up trap with compartments. This technological wonder aligns one compartment at a time with the outside world. When a mouse steps inside, a clockwork mechanism moves the enclosed merry-go-round a notch, which traps the mouse and lines the next and empty compartment up with the door. The idea, apparently, is to get a full house, then tie a string to the handle and immerse the whole contraption in a bucket of water. Ah, but the drowning act is a subsequent and separate activity. It is, happily, an option. It is entirely possible to trap a lot of mice and not drown them. With nothing but their rodent dignity and best-laid plans awry, they can be transported into benevolent exile. Every mouse should have its Elba.

I purchased the trap and in a moment of largesse baited it with very good ripe Brie. Our captives' last meal on our premises could be memorable, at least. They could remember us fondly if not for our enduring hospitality at least for style.

A quick visit to the laundry the next morning revealed a single victim in the first compartment to have moved beyond access to the single door. I had him! His fate had been calculated in advance. Across the road from our house then (the road intersected our drive exactly ninety-six feet from our house) was a common, a few acres of woods heavily overgrown with brush and windfall trees, a veritable paradise where a wild mouse could raise its family in any of ten thousand dens and crevices, a place of tunnels and safety, a wholly secret place whose brambles would discourage dogs and all but the most determined of cats. It was safe haven, and I was certain any mice transported there would understand immediately and perhaps in their own way appreciate their entry upon good times.

Trap in hand, I made my way well into the bramble thicket at some considerable risk to my legs and ankles and unscrewed the wing nut that turned the compartments into wee little mouse dungeons. I gently tipped my prisoner out onto a fallen tree and to my amazement saw the creature shoot straight back between my feet, disappear under a bush, and reappear on the far side heading straight for the edge of the road. It shot across the tarmac into the gaping maw of our driveway, making unerringly for the house. It had learned nothing and certainly did not appreciate my efforts on its behalf. Unfortunately neither the mouse nor I had taken people watching by cats into account. Of our then ten resident cats, seven were sitting shoulder to shoulder across the centre of the driveway. By the time the mouse saw the line of scrimmage it was too late to veer and it was mercifully over in a moment. I don't know who actually got him but I suspect half-wild Omari, a white and marmalade job that lived with us because there was nowhere else for him to go. He was born to a feral mother and by the time he met people for the first time, it was too late. He trusted his wits but nothing and no one else. And he was a murderous animal around potential prey. A mouse coming straight at him would have been light work.

The cats thought the mouse-release game was the best thing to come along since cow's milk and hung around hopefully mewing, I am sure, *"Do it again, Daddy, more, more more."* Future successfully trapped mice were driven to a spot about a half a mile away, but until we moved from that house, if I walked out of the front door one or more cats would follow me, particularly if I went to the end of the drive to check the letter-box. There was always a chance I would release another mouse or two. The cats watched me. There was absolutely no doubt about it. One or more soon joined by others would appear in the driveway, sit down facing the road, and wait to see what wonderful thing I would do next.

There is an added fillip to the mouse-release game I inadvertently invented that summer day years ago. New cats joined us after that and they watched, too. I can't believe the old-timers *told* them about that great day when I triggered a mousy free-for-all. That would be a bit much even for me, and I can't accept contagion as the answer, either. The only explanation I can come up with is that cats watch cats that are people watching and decide there has to be something to it. Now, exactly what is it our cats see?

2

Certain assumptions have to be made when you are dealing with anything as arcane as a cat. The simplest is that a cat has an array of sensors and systems that we can relate to. Each sense is an avenue leading inward from the outside world, an entrance for information, and however rich a cat's internal life may be it does have to eat and duck things, hide and seek a variety of gratifications. We know, and need not assume, that they can see, they can hear, they can smell, they can taste, and they can feel—that is, they have the sense of touch. But it is downright presumptuous for us to believe that they do these things rather as we do them or to compare how they do them with our own five parallel faculties. It may not matter a bit that cats hear better than we do or that their sense of smell is less acute or more acute or as acute as our own. When we come to the senses of the cat, we should at least try to think of them as the cat's alone and function—uncharacteristically for human beings—without judgement. If we need an occasional yardstick we will have to accept that. But it is for measuring, not judging. We shall neither smirk nor shall we know envy. That may be difficult to do. The only comparative measure we understand at all is our own cluster of senses. So be it.

Now the assumption part. We are not being particularly far-out or "spooky" nor are we walking at the edge of other worlds when we at least acknowledge that cats may have other avenues into the reality of their space and time. Lots of people claim to have a sixth sense and surely if there can be a sixth sense, there can be a seventh, an eighth, or a tenth. There is not one whit of logic in assuming there can exist only one sense beyond the five we generally acknowledge. For all we know, there can be thirty-six more. Since we can't define the sixth one so many of us believe is a part of reality, why should we be able to define any number of others? Even to acknowledge that a sixth sense might exist is to open a sensory floodgate and to take the consequence. The worst we can do is admit to profound ignorance.

We are going to work with the five senses we allow both the cat and ourselves first, then wonder (explore *would* be presumptuous) about what might lie beyond. Not to frighten anyone off but rather to give a little advance notice of what we could be getting into, allow me to speak of a sense we often claim for ourselves—precognition. I believe some of us are precognitive. The phone rings, we say that is "old So-and-So" although old So-and-so has been out of our lives for months or perhaps years, and by golly, it *is* old So-and-So. Millions of us, I am sure, have had things like that happen so often that denial is useless. It does happen and all of it cannot be explained away with convenient brush-offs in the nature of *coincidence, imagination, hysteria, mistaken impression, conversion reaction, attention getting, forgotten or overlooked legitimate forewarning, theatrical stunt, prevarication, a lobotomy hangover, an effort to appear interesting,* or by simply saying it isn't so. Why we go to such lengths to prove that we don't know something is beyond me. Not to know something and to admit it is like an invitation to the ball. It means we can go on to explore perhaps wonderful new things. Nothing could possibly be duller than knowing it all. Fortunately that is not a threat we have to deal with. It is not scheduled to happen soon.

Some years ago we lived in England and I had several encounters with one of the better minds of our time. Professor I. J. Good of Oxford has been one of this century's key contributors to the art and science of both physics and statistics. He is also one of England's greatest cryptoanalysts, or codebreakers. Jack normally dwells intellectually where most of the rest of us would be afraid to go if we had any idea how to get there, and a good thing that is, too. The things he has thought about and the things he has published are so confoundingly profound that people are generally loath to ignore anything he says. There is that phenomenon in the way we relate to ideas. An Einstein says that if you launch a clock at the speed of light, time will not register because time will not have passed during the clock's journey. Let any of the rest of us try to sell an idea like that and see how far we get!

Anyway, back to Jack Good. He hasn't gone into clocks in my presence, but precious few other things have escaped his very high-level notice. One evening we were assaulting a couple of fillets of plaice, as I recall, and generally dissecting the world and our place in it, when somehow precognition came up and I asked him if he had ever thought much about it. Without hesitation he acknowledged that he had had many such experiences himself and startled me by saying the explanation was really quite simple. I would not have thought that could be the case but leaned forward to gather in what was bound to be startling new information for the likes of me. Geniuses are always fun to listen to even if you can't sleep that night or it all gives you a headache.

"We have found," he said in his cultured Oxford tones, "that there are subatomic particles that move around the nuclei of their respective atoms in the wrong direction. They are speeding at unbelievable rates against the mainstream of particles of matter so much smaller than the atoms of which they are part that we can barely imagine them. Exactly why they don't have head-on collisions is not clear."

I had been wondering about things as simple and uncosmic as guessing who was calling before answering the phone and had not yet made the connection with atomic physics that I was obviously going to be expected to make at any moment. I leaned forward even further. We were getting into heavy stuff and one always has an obligation when dining with geniuses to appear not only interested but in tune with what they are saying. They know your limitations full well but they are usually at least trying to tone it down. I feel I should at least try to keep up with them.

"Now," Jack continued, "if the basic building blocks of matter itself can run backwards, for that is what they are surely doing, so can time. It has to be so. When you are precognitive, you are simply remembering the future."

As of this writing I have had twenty-three years to play with that, and although I can hear his voice still and recall his words almost verbatim I am not sure I am one whit closer to understanding what he said now than I was then. But to the point: can that be applied to the cats?

I have written elsewhere (*A Celebration of Cats*) of a black cat called Tom. He didn't belong to us and in fact we never knew where he came from, but he took to hanging around our place, mingling easily with our own cats and our dogs. He took a special fix on our daughter Pamela, who was then a college student. That in itself was not unusual because most animals take to Pamela as if she were St. Francis. Animals that will not go near another human being, feral dogs and cats, obstreperous horses that are homicidal with anyone else, they all home in on Pamela and literally eat out of her hand. And so it was with Tom. He was a perfectly pleasant animal with everyone else, animal or human, but Pamela was at the centre of his universe, at least when she was around. The mystery lay in the fact that he was around only when she was.

Tom would come when Pamela was home for a long weekend or a holiday and then vanish the moment she went back to school. We never found him casing our place or checking us out. Somehow he knew in other ways, and when Pamela was away, so was he.

Now this is where it gets spooky. When Pamela was due home, almost invariably Tom (we called him that for obvious reasons) would be sitting on the front steps or at the end of the driveway waiting as she pulled in in her car. It happened far too often to be coincidence. He never once appeared when Pamela was not due. Somehow the cat, whose actual identity and home we never learned, would know when Pamela was driving the two hundred or so miles from her campus in New Jersey. He would come from wherever he came and be there before she arrived. I am not certain Pamela fully accepted the idea that he was only on hand when she was due, but there are many witnesses to that truth.

We had no other black cats at the time so mistaken identity isn't a possibility. When Tom was there you knew it. He came into the house at mealtime with our own regular feline herd and there is no overlooking a

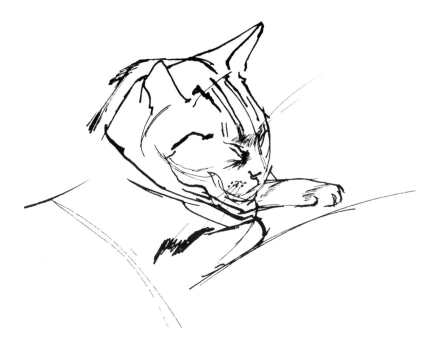

very large, full-faced, jet black tom that curls up on a chair or couch and waits for his one and only true love. At times he never even made it into the house. He cut it so close that it was only minutes before Pamela appeared that Tom would take up his station outside.

It is difficult to ascribe Tom's repeated accomplishment to seeing, hearing, smelling, tasting, or touch. There was nothing to see, hear, smell, taste, or touch when Tom materialised out of nowhere after being absent for weeks or months. Can time run backwards for cats as well as people? Was Tom remembering the good times with Pamela he was going to have when he made his way to our house? Or could he see or hear or smell, taste or touch Pamela getting into her car two hundred miles away and sense the way in which she was driving?

But, first, the five obvious senses we can detect and demonstrate because we have them, too. A cat's primary sense is sight, and it has very efficient eyes designed to facilitate the work and survival of a night hunter. First, its eyes are large when compared with the size of its head. If our eyes were as large in comparison to our heads, we would have something midway between a softball and a bowling ball looming over each cheek. That is unpleasant to contemplate, but the cat, because its eyes look forward, has somewhat the look of a baby primate and we find that appealing. The cat's eyes are mysterious to us. More has been written about them than about the eyes of any other animal. When was the last time you heard of a semi-precious mineral named for a rhinoceros's eyes or a poem written about the orbs of a wombat? We have looked back at cats, into their eyes, and we have wondered about secrets and other special things.

The cat eye is spherical in shape and not particularly remarkable in basic structure. Out front is the protective window called the cornea. Nothing unusual about that. Centred behind the cornea is a variable opening called the pupil; through it light passes to the lens and from there converges on the retina at the rear of the eye. There are two important elements in the cat's eye which enable the animal to function in special ways and which have given rise to a lot of nonsense fables. First, the pupil.

The cat is not able to adjust or focus the lenses in its eyes or to alter the shape of the eyes themselves, which may mean somewhat fuzzy vision, at least in the middle of a field. Ah, but that pupil. In reduced light, the pupil expands into a vast circle practically filling the eye. Very little else shows when the pupil is fully open. As light intensifies, the pupil narrows down to a vertical slit, not a smaller circle. The lion, essentially a day hunter, has pupils that narrow to almost pinpoints, but they are round. Not our companion cat. Not only does the narrow slit control the light passing in to the lens but the cat's eyelids move up and down at right angles to the slitlike pupil, so in effect a cat squinting has both horizontal and vertical controls. That allows the cat's eye to be very much more sensitive to light than animals who do their work during the day. That extreme sensitivity is most valuable when the lights are low. But without those fine controls on the quantity or intensity of the light admitted, a cat couldn't function at all during bright daylight. As we all know, cats do, very well indeed.

At the back of the eye the retina is covered with ten highly reflective layers of zinc and several highly evolved proteins. It has been called a mirrored patch but is technically known as the *tapetum lucidum*. That literally translates as "bright carpet". It is a highly refined image intensifier. Every scrap of light coming onto the cornea, through the pupil to the lens and thence to the retina, is transmitted to the brain. In the dark the cat has excellent vision but there is the nonsense tale about cats seeing

in the absence of light. Cats see in absolute darkness just exactly what we see in absolute darkness, absolutely nothing. However, there is darkness and there is darkness, and here we have to make a comparison. Our eyes respond to what we like to think of as the visible spectrum. We do not see ultraviolet rays but cats do, and they almost certainly see some other parts of the band that we can detect only with instruments.

That *tapetum lucidum* on the retina is what makes the cat's eyes glow at night when struck by a direct beam of artificial light (which makes it tough on photographers using flash bulbs or a strobe). The cat's eyes appear iridescent, and if the glow is yellow-green or blue-green the cat almost certainly has gold or copper eyes. A cat with blue eyes will appear as two burning red balls when picked up by our headlights.

Typical of the predator, the cat's eyes have a great deal of overlap in their fields, giving the hunter its necessary binocular vision. That allows the cat's brain to make very accurate assessments and judgements in varying terrain and assures the cat of a safe landing place as it climbs and jumps. A clumsy cat probably has eye problems, or something related to the ear, as we shall discuss in the next chapter. Cats enhance their vision by special behaviour. A cat about to pounce from one tree limb to another or upon a hapless mouse is likely to sway its head from side to side. That gives the animal's brain an opportunity to make a final and extremely refined assessment of distance, before the action takes place. The closer a cat is to its prey or landing place, the greater the displacement caused by the head-swaying trick. Cats are accurate animals. They are designed to be. Since cats need only about one sixth of the amount of light we do to see quite well, the head swaying is used at any time of the day or night when precision is needed. Cats appear to take their extraordinary accuracy for granted. When a cat misses, it looks downright amazed. A cat that falls sulks.

Again a necessary comparison, necessary for a frame of reference. Cats have far better peripheral vision that we do. We mentioned above that a cat's vision may be somewhat blurred at the centre of the field because their lenses and eye shape are fixed (and they lack a device, a kind of indentation, known as the fovea). That is compensated for by the acuity at the edges of their field of vision and by compensations their brains automatically make. Of course head swaying at critical moments at the leading edge of action also plays an important role. Just how great is a cat's field of vision? About 120 degrees of overlap or binocular vision straight ahead, plus 80 degrees of monocular vision on each side. That comes out to 280 degrees. For 80 degrees of a complete circle, 2/9 of the whole, a cat is blind, and that blacked-out area is centred on the cat's tail. A hunter needs that binocular vision out in front where the stalking is going to take place. It is less concerned about what is going on behind it. Its prey, however, can't take that kind of risk. Its vision is panoramic. That is usually true among the higher animals.

Movement is terribly important to a cat—it is the great stimulator. Some movements are much more stimulating than others and nothing works quite as well as an object of jumpable size moving away. For cats, that is virtually impossible to resist. Something going across their field of vision is interesting enough, but not necessarily totally captivating. If mice could learn to run in tight circles, cats would probably watch them with fascination, but would be far less likely to pounce. Not even

Drawings by Theophile-Alexandre Steinlen

evolution, the great adjuster, is likely to teach mice that secret, however. Of course *ever* is a very long time. The mouse of the distant future might be a circler or at least run zigzag on the diagonal.

Whether or not cats see colour has engendered an enormous amount of controversy. We have gone through several "they see only in shades of grey" generations of scientists and have at last come to the point where we can say without fear of ridicule, *Yes, cats see colours as colours.*

Cat eyes are equipped with an enormous number of structures called rods which are very easily stimulated and work well for night hunters but which do not distinguish colours. Conelike structures are the ones that are sensitive to various wavelengths. It is now pretty well accepted that cats can distinguish between the following pairs of colours:

> red and green
> red and blue
> red and grey
> green and blue
> green and grey
> blue and grey
> yellow and blue
> yellow and grey

and tests are still going on to see if they can separate red from yellow.

That limited list of distinctions a cat can make plus the relatively low cone-to-rod count in their eyes' structure probably means cats do not see the fine display we do when we walk through a garden or a museum gallery. They do, however, see as much colour as they need to see, and they do see things five or six times as brightly as we do, so it has apparently been sorted out pretty well by their own evolution.

There is one other bit of structure relating to the eye that we should note: the nictating membrane. This is a third eyelid, really, under the two outer ones. It moves from the inside corner of the eye horizontally across to the outside edge. It is not part of the light-control mechanism that the up and down outer lids are, so its role is probably simply added protection.

We mentioned fables that have grown up around the eye of the cat and there are a lot of them. Samples: you can tell the time of day by looking at the shape of a cat's pupils, so variable are the openings. If that were true, you could control the time of day with a strong flashlight, but it makes a nice story which, strangely, is still widely believed. Another good one is the idea that a cat's eyes shine at night because they are casting out the light they absorbed during the day. According to some cultures, the phases of the moon can be calculated by looking into a cat's eyes, and those slits-to-circles coincide with the tides. Of course it is inevitable that the Devil get into the act, and so we have it that the night shine of the cat's eyes represents the fires of Hell. That belief could explain a lot of rubbish in human behaviour towards cats. It would all be quaint and mildly amusing, in fact, if the people who really have believed these things had not been murderous cat haters. Fear, after all, generates hate as nothing else does.

In the years before the American Civil War when blacks in the South were denied virtually any form of education, superstition had to take the place of knowledge. They believed that cats could see ghosts and that ghost visions were reflected in their eyes. That could put one off cats, I suppose. They killed cats, sad to report, and used their eyes in voodoo charms. They also used cats' whiskers for their magic, but that did not require sacrificing cats, just making them furious.

In fact, though, a cat's eyes do exactly what most eyes do. They absorb radiant energy whatever the source, convert that energy to chemicals, which in turn become electrical energy that goes to the animal's brain. It is in its brain that the cat actually sees us. That is where the image is formed and there the animal's memory resides, and it is from there that its response to our image will come. What we have no way of knowing is how much of that response is reflex and how much is "considered". I suspect rather less of the latter in most instances.

Cats very often sit or lie and stare straight ahead with what we think of as a blank expression. That probably has to do with the relatively dim image they get, in the centre of their field of vision. Let something move into their peripheral zones, however, particularly with spastic or jerky motions, and the responses all start up in sequence. The tail flicks, denoting a heightened level of interest, the chin sinks, the ears flatten out, and in extreme cases the lower jaw begins to chatter or pulse. That chattering action is quite possibly an imitation of the cat's killing bite. It is anticipating getting whatever is in view by the back of the neck and severing its spinal cord. No matter how a cat may feel about us humans as individuals or how vocal the cat is, it never uses that chattering sound to comment on us directly. We can at times elicit the response by doing things like dragging or tossing a small object, but the cat will not react to us that way directly. We are biteable, but not bite-size.

How do cats see and react to us? We are large and do not as total beings elicit any pounce reactions. A hand can, if moved back and forth in front of a cat, and a foot can, if jiggled, become a practice session target, but a whole human being must be a little awesome. Our skin is not particularly colourful and since we are without real fur and certainly without feathers, our clothing must supply any colour display a cat can distinguish. We are, then, more or less stimulating to the cones of a cat's eye (depending on what we are wearing), but distinctly interesting to the rods. Either way we are visually notable, if pretty grey in the flesh.

Most of us move fairly smoothly. We are not all Fred Astaires, but sitting, standing, reaching, or walking, our actions have fairly discreet beginnings, middles, and ends. When we perform certain tasks, winding wool, sweeping the floor, or sorting strawberries, our actions can become a little jerky and therefore far more interesting to a cat. If a cat is not hungry or not in need of a little rubbing—scratching, patting, or rubbing to a cat is a sign of unending, in fact unendable infancy in relation to their human owners; mothers lick their kittens and our petting actions are from the cat's point of view an imitation of that highly desirable sensation—we are probably pretty ordinary visual experiences. We are large, impossible to miss for an animal as acutely sensitive to its surroundings as a cat. So we almost never manage to surprise them. They do, after all, combine their vision with their other sensory cluster, and we would have to loom large.

The important thing in speculating how a cat sees us—"see" in this case meaning its total reaction to us as stimulators and not just things literally seen by the eyes—is to remember the amount of emotional baggage a cat carries. They are intelligent animals, probably on a level with dogs and pigs, and very sensitive. They are also high-strung much of the time when they are fully awake because they are predators. Predators store up kinetic energy by sleeping or napping a lot of the time. That enables them to perform Herculean tasks when the situation calls upon them to do so. A leopard can carry prey nearly as heavy as it is itself up a tree. That is because of stored energy. And that same energy is evident in our house cats as well. Being high-strung and very intelligent are sure signs of an animal that can be, in fact must be, conditioned by early experiences.

If a kitten is picked up, cuddled, and carried around several times a day from its first day of life, it will be a very different animal as an adult from a cat that is rarely if ever touched until it is eight or nine weeks old. In fact, cats that are not handled at all until they are two or three months old may be totally unmanageable as pets. Omari was referred to earlier. Whatever Omari sees when he sees a human being is not safe or promising; he virtually never allows anyone to touch him. He flees at the sight of a man. Omari was probably never handled. When his mother was trapped and destroyed for killing too many birds at the farmer's bird-feeding station, Omari was also caught and given to a shelter. He could not be adopted out because he was all but untouchable, so we took him in.

Surely that kind of conditioning has a great deal to do with how a cat sees us. As suggested when we discussed the origins of Squid, the nature of that conditioning is generally indecipherable except in terms of how comfortable a cat seems around people, dogs, and other cats. In almost all cases a human being and even a dog is easier for a cat to accommodate than another cat. That harks back to territoriality, which in turn means food supply (the "hunting block" of the tiger) and sexual opportunity.

So, to sum up about vision, cats see us pretty clearly, judging from the

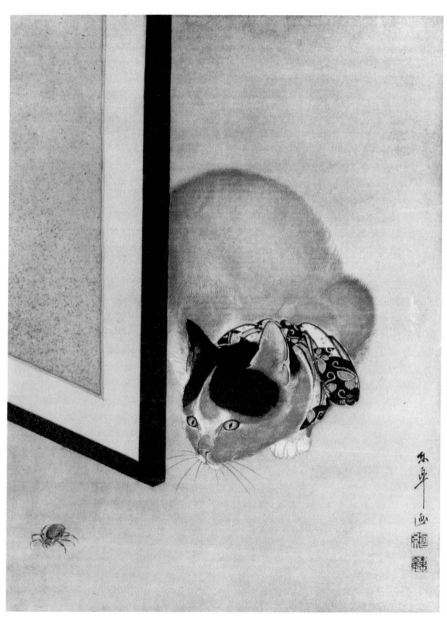

Cat watching a spider, by Toko

nature of the equipment they carry. We are perhaps blurred giants when seen straight on, clearer near the edges of the field of vision. We are colourful, literally, if we are wearing colourful clothing. We are undoubtedly in proper perspective with the objects around us—a cat that couldn't judge relative size couldn't hunt, climb, or leap. Clearly a cat would not survive long if it couldn't tell a mouse from a Great Dane when it went out hunting. In fact they probably see us pretty much as we are.

We tend to move, so cats watch us. We often provide extra food opportunities, and so cats watch us. We generally provide elements of their regular diet, so cats watch us. Cats have an absolute imperative to survey their turf and check for intruders, and we are the door openers and door closers in their lives, the only ones they do know—so cats watch us. We imitate their mother's licking and cleaning when we pet them, and that has to feel wonderful since being infantile provides nice sensations in cats as well as ourselves, so cats watch us. When we are not moving, when we are in repose, there is always the chance we will pat them and let them be infants again, as they want to be.

Add to those factors two others, one we have mentioned and one we haven't. We spoke of the emotional baggage any intelligent animal brings to every situation, the conditioning, and besides, we are peculiar beasts who do things no cat could ever understand. We turn on taps and television, we engage in sporting activities, we sit and face each other and make funny sounds, we bathe (willingly get wet!), shave, shampoo, cook, hang pictures, move furniture around, make sounds into an instrument, go again and again to the door but never patrol territory, and have one of the strangest-looking litter trays any creature has ever seen. As intelligent animals, cats are curious. They also do not want to be caught off guard by huge creatures (if you are of medium weight and build you weigh eighteen to twenty times as much as your cat and a man may easily stand twelve times as high). No cat in its right mind would not watch us. To sum up a summation—many of the best things in life and many of the worst come from us. Why shouldn't cats watch us?

3

Cats and humans live in a highly flexible medium, and the ability of an animal to detect changes in that medium—that is, vibrations—is essential to its survival. Sensitivity to rapidly repeated changes or cycles of touch is what we call hearing. Awareness of fluid-borne or earth-borne vibrations would not be qualitatively different as long as the receiver of the information had the ability to get it to his brain for evaluation and response without appreciable delay. Cat ears are complicated organs that evolved from organs of balance and they are in that regard in the mainstream of mammalian evolution. Like all their fellow mammals they still use what have become hearing devices for balance. Balance is slightly more critical in cats than in many other mammals because cats climb and jump so much and often so precariously, at least from our point of view. However, an elephant with vertigo would be as awesome as it would be pitiful. Let us acknowledge that balance and the ability to detect and evaluate sounds are of singular importance to all animals evolved to have them. And all of that happens in the same place.

Hearing is basically the same in a cat as in most other mammals. A wave of pressure changes bombards the animal. The waves strike the outer ears or pinnae (singular, pinna), which are really skin- and fur-covered plates of cartilage. The pinna (also known as the auricle) is designed to collect sound waves and direct them downward into a resonating channel toward the eardrum. To accomplish all of this the pinnae are cone-shaped, upstanding (in virtually all breeds except the relatively recent and very attractive mutation known as the Scottish fold), and very flexible. Those pinnae are much more efficient than our flat, close-to-the-head, inflexible cup handles. But, then, we are not anywhere near as closely attuned to our environment as the cat is. We don't hunt with our teeth and our forefeet.

Each of the cat's pinna has over twenty muscles and can be rotated through an arc of a little over 180 degrees. And we consider someone who can wiggle their ears even a bit gifted, at least in that regard. A cat would sneer.

Once the sound has been directed downward by the sweeping pinna, it bounces back and forth off the ridges inside the pinna and picks up further distinguishing characteristics. The cat adds to its sonar/radarlike capabilities by moving its head, pointing one or both ears towards a source of sound origin even when it cannot pick up any additional signals as to where that might be. In a sense, it reaches out to follow the vibrations to their beginnings. Since the cat's two ears are separated by a fairly broad skull, there is a tiny split-second difference in the timing of a vibration's arrival and there may be distinct variations in its intensity. All of these data are processed and used as locators. A cat can detect about five degrees difference in source location. Probably because our heads are so much larger and separate our ears that much more we can get that differentiation down to about three degrees, but that is the only way our hearing is more precise than that of a cat.

Once the sound waves have passed down through the resonating outer chamber and hit the vibrating eardrum, they enter a fluid-filled middle ear and roll along through three linked bones. At last they arrive at the labyrinthine inner ear and are passed off to auditory receptor cells for transmission to the brain. Incoming vibrations have then been trans-muted into nerve impulses, and once those impulses have reached the brain, the animal can be said to have heard. That inward transmission involves an incredible series of changes as mechanical movement becomes electrical and then chemical then electrical again thousands of times over—and all of it virtually instantaneous. Although parts of the whole like the pinna can react on their own to vibrations, hearing, like seeing, occurs in the brain and nowhere else.

How well does a cat hear? Very, very acutely. Their lower register probably starts where ours does at about 20 cycles a second. We go up to about 20,000 cycles when we are young, which is about where the high notes on a violin vibrate. But our auditory nerve bundle has only about thirty thousand fibres in it and a cat's has a third again as many. Those

forty thousand fibres raise the cat's upper-cycle limit to approximately 50,000 cycles, leaving us far behind. The cat is nowhere near the top, however. A mouse hears up to 95,000 cycles, bats up to 120,000, and porpoises, the absolute champions, receive signals they can distinguish at 150,000 cycles and perhaps a bit higher than that. Still, cats hear more than well enough for what their lifestyle demands.

There is a theory about another aspect of cat hearing, although I am not certain of it. It suggests that the extremely fine hairs around the opening of the cat's outer chamber are subject to incessant movements that the cat can hear and that that is the bottom threshold of their hearing. Perhaps, and perhaps not, but it is known that that fringe of hair on the pinna at the bottom helps keep wind-borne debris from entering the ear and compromising the cat's hearing. Perhaps that hair has additional uses as well. Not very much that grows on a cat is extraneous or wasted.

The size of the ear indicates to some degree the origin of the breed (all domestic cats belong to the same species). The pinna is an important means of heat loss, so larger pinnae represent temperate to tropical origins and could function as they do in elephants, as cooling mechanisms. (There is no proof of that yet, however.) Small pinnae like those found in the Persian cat support the theory of a steppe cat origin for that breed. An interesting aspect of cat ears is that cats do not usually get car-sick the way dogs do, although their ears are very similar. Motion sickness originates in the internal ear, and no one has yet figured out what cats have that dogs do not have, or vice versa. It is likely to be linked to their fine sense of balance. Most cats hate riding in cars but it is apparently not because they are nauseous.

Cats are not precocious at birth—they are atricocius, which means their ears and eyes are sealed and non-functional. Their sense of smell has to cover those early necessary bases for them until about the middle of their second week, when their eyes and ears start opening and they discover there is a whole new world beyond. Cats never stop investigating that world once they learn it is there. It is a source of unending joy and very challenging.

Cats communicate in often complex ways and sound has its role in their interactions with each other. It is true, as we shall see, that they communicate by scent and certainly by posture, but they also use sound, and their ears obviously must have a part to play. Cats hiss and spit when they are upset, pushed a little too far or when they sense their territory has been intruded upon. Why a hiss, why a spit? The suggestion is—and although it is logical, I find it difficult to think of it as more than a suggestion—they make those sounds in mimicry of a snake. Just about all animals recognise that some snakes are best left alone; the theory is that cats produce the same threat sounds to earn the same respect. It has been stated so often that it has almost taken on the stamp of truth. Yet lions and tigers, leopards and puma, all hiss and spit too. Does a tiger earn survival advantages or a leopard brownie points by imitating a snake? In my own mind I have to leave room for reasonable doubt. (As far as safety and survival goes, I can't see much difference between being locked in a phone booth with an angry leopard or a waspish king cobra.)

Cats purr, and no one is really certain why, although there have been more than enough theories presented as fact. It starts when kittens nurse and it has been stated many times that purring is a cat's way of showing contentment. The mother on which those kittens are nursing during their first purrs is also purring in all likelihood, but she also purred while she was in labour. She will purr when sick and even when injured. She will be likely to purr while she is dying unless it is sudden. Contentment just doesn't seem to do it. Profundity seems to have something to do with it. When cats are profoundly anything, contented, in pain, in any form of extremis, they seem to purr. Beyond that, it is something of a mystery.

Cats cannot roar but they can growl. They can scream with pain and rage and make a sound variously described as *mew, meow* and *miaow*. Put a lot of that together and you have what some people call caterwauling. That does convey the experience pretty well.

Back in 1944 a study was done suggesting that cats actually use nine consonants, five vowels, two diphthongs, and one triphthong. Add to these variations in volume, pitch, and intensity and you have a pretty good working vocabulary. In their various calls and cries cats can convey the finer points of anger, warning (both *Watch out friend* and *Stay away foe*), surprise, sexual invitation, sexual satisfaction, pain, protest, pleading, excitement, concern, and complaint. And perhaps that many descriptions of their world and their own moods again. That does suggest they need ears to hear each other because it is with each other they are most often communicating. We must remember that when we talk of our house cats, they deal with us as one of their own once they accept us by becoming a part of our family, so "each other" is perfectly correct.

But cat-to-cat communication is only part of it and probably the smaller part as well. Cats are night hunters, we may recall, and it is true that their eyesight is remarkable in very reduced light. Still, they have to be able to locate things in order to see them. A cat in a barn full of bales of hay and sacks of feed can't see through, around, or over obstacles many times its own size. Sight, no matter how good, can't reach out and find a potential meal. A pinna rotating over half a circle's worth of arc and picking up sounds so high and soft we could never detect them can do exactly that. The cat's brain can then guide it to an advantageous position and then the eyes can be brought into play to their full advantage. It is true that a mouse walking on straw can alert a cat; it is probably true that a cat

can tell its owner's automobile engine from other cars of the same make and year, and a cat can certainly hear footsteps far down the driveway.

A cat can hear dogs walking. It can hear its owner open a refrigerator (I am prepared to demonstrate that to any doubters as many times as they wish). A cat can capture, relay to its brain, identify, and issue commands for reaction to sounds that would be astounding for us to experience. They have demonstrated what is apparently a sensitivity to vibrations acute enough to foretell earthquakes and volcanic activity well in advance of a happening.

What do they hear from us? I would suspect a great deal of noise they simply can't interpret. When people talk to each other they don't use the falsetto and other affectations they use with cats, so I imagine human-to-human conversation is so much background clutter, as are telephones ringing and dogs barking. We had a cat, a Siamese now gone, who did not like the sound of a telephone ringing. It was inevitably met with a punishing *miaow* whenever it went off. She felt the same way about alarm clocks. We can speculate and wonder if those sounds were uncomfortable for her, but I don't think so. We have never had another cat carry on about telephones so I suspect it was simply her comment on sounds she did not enjoy, or perhaps it was because she couldn't put them into any sensible context. There is always the possibility that they were a kind of mechanical *miaow* to which she was simply responding.

A friend has a cat that miaows when a phone rings and keeps it up until it is answered. An answered phone stops ringing and if a cat doesn't like the sound why not demand relief? We do not know and probably will never be able to evaluate each bit of unique behaviour we encounter with cats. They are assertively singular animals and we have no reasonable avenues to their thoughts. The cat brain, interestingly enough, speaking of thoughts, is very much like our own. The great big cortex, a recent area to evolve, where we store memories, is missing, and a large bulbous area for speech patterns in the older part of the brain is much smaller in proportion, but otherwise the two brains are similar.

Back to that falsetto. When we want to retrieve a cat or summon a cat or just get a cat's attention, we typically raise our voices by several octaves and repeat the one word *kitty* very rapidly over and over again. The well-known cat and dog photographer Walter Chandoha had fourteen cats and one dog when I visited his home, and he and his wife had named the dog Kitty. That made it much easier, he said, when it was feeding time. He or his wife simply went to the back door and gave the good old *kitty-kitty-kitty* call and all fifteen animals came running. We don't generally use a falsetto or other "cute" voice trick when we talk to our dogs but we very often do when we commune with our cats. I suspect that is because of the way we perceive the cat's voice. We are trying to be kittylike ourselves. It probably also has to do with the fact that we never allow our cats to grow up. We almost always use diminutives like *kitty*, *pussy*, and *puss* when we refer to them, unless they have done something bad like used the laundry basket for a restroom or knocked a Tang horse off the mantelpiece. Only then do most of us refer to "the cat".

Cats do know their own names, I am convinced. We had a lynx-point Siamese named Kate. She was one of the sweetest, least contentious animals I have ever known. She was Earth Mother. She wanted to bathe every dog, cat, and human she met—endlessly. She did have a peculiarity about her name. If you said upon encountering her, "Kate, are you a bad cat?" she would give you a resounding *niaowww* in return. And it was an *nnnnnn* sound and not her usual *mmmmmm*-sound *miaow*. I am not going to insist it was a negative response, but I will insist it was a response to her name. Any other expression using the same tone of voice failed to attract her attention. The same expression without the "Kate" similarly drew a blank. I am quite certain Kate understood her own name although perhaps not the other words. Perhaps it is silly to argue points like that. After you have exhausted yourself, you find you still have converted no one and even in your own mind it remains a question mark.

Although it is quite certain cats hear us in ways we can't even hear ourselves or each other, we are probably not all that rewarding to listen to, nowhere near as much fun as we are to watch. There are cats that like to lie on the chests of people they love, whether the people are lying down or sitting up. They often rest their heads against their human friend's face and neck. It is quite likely they can hear blood in the carotid artery and that the blood thumping its way towards the brain is a real pulse and comforting to the cat. That is one of the places a cat would be likely to bite you if you were mouse-sized and it was hungry. Not wanting to bite you there as expressed by cuddling up and listening to the target may be a way of expressing friendship, and the human partner in the exercise may in fact be inadvertently expressing a measure of submission. It is really very difficult to put these things together as anything but conjecture. However, when a cat is lying on your chest it certainly picks up your heartbeat. That can be comforting since as a foetus the cat felt (not heard) its mother's heartbeat. With young kittens that do not have a mother to care for them, it is kind to wrap a nice noisy kitchen clock (obviously the wind-up kind) in a towel and put it in their box with them. You will find them cuddling it, reassured by its semblance to the ticking they felt *in utero*.

Human beings filter sound. Clearly we would go mad if we listened to every voice and every mechanical sound we are capable of hearing. We generally are able automatically to filter out all but the most intrusive sounds if we don't need them at the moment. We do not know if the cats we have invited to share our lives and therefore our cacophony filter it, too. If they don't, life must be very noisy for them. As far as we know, cats can't shut off their ears completely. To some extent they learn to accept sounds even if they can't actually filter them. A cat raised with dogs knows her own dogs' barks. A good healthy *woof-woof* that would put an uninitiated cat up a tree won't draw any response at all from a cat that is used to that particular dog.

Although cats nap a great deal they also sleep deeply. Very often I have seen one or more cats sleeping soundly in our living room and watched them wake up almost in unison. One after another they have got up, walked across the living room, into and across the dining room, and out into and across a hall. Once at the far wall, which is mostly glass, they have jumped up on chairs and looked down onto bird feeders that have suddenly become busy. The feeders are below the bottoms of the hall windows and the cats were truly asleep, often with their backs to the windows two rooms away. Unless they were using a sense we don't know about, they must have heard the birds. Since birds nest all over our heavily planted garden and are always chirping and peeping and trilling their territorial claims, what the cats had to have heard through the veil of their sleep were the sounds of feathered flight or small extra calls birds may make en route to feed. I can't hear it so I am only suggesting it might be there. If cats sleeping can hear that change in the sounds in the garden, what can a fully alerted cat on the prowl hear? They can penetrate and interact with a world we hardly know is there—and quite possibly levels or even worlds beyond that.

How well cats understand sounds that come to them from our gadget-filled world is difficult to interpret, much less how they might be able to use them to their own advantage. I know a woman named Christine who has a cat with one of the strangest behavioural patterns I have encountered this side of the edge of reality. She installed a television set in her bedroom, the kind with the push-pull buttons for ON and OFF. Simply, there is a little plastic button on the control panel beside the screen and when it is pulled out you have television. One morning at five-thirty (!), shortly after she installed the box, she was awakened by the terribly disturbing sound of someone counting, very loudly. It was an early morning exercise show, a hideous assault on a sensitive mind. She was alone in her apartment with her cat, who was now sitting on top of the television console looking smug.

"All right," she said, once the panic had subsided and she was somewhat in control, "I might as well feed you."

It was a fatal error. She reinforced her cat's behaviour by rewarding him for committing a dastardly act. Now, unless she remembers to crawl around on her hands and knees and pull out the wall plug before she goes to bed, she can be reasonably certain of a five-thirty wake-up call. I suggested turning the sound down to zero but have not checked to see if it works. Perhaps the flickering light will wake her, too.

Does the cat understand that it can access sleep-disturbing sound clutter and thereby get fed early by hanging down over the face of a television set and pulling a button with its teeth? Apparently. There is a lot of complex baggage that goes into that series of acts, events, and results, however, and dragging one's feet before answering is allowed. In fact, it is recommended.

Cats are such meticulous animals it is difficult to imagine how they tolerate our sound clutter—radio, television, stereos with enough power to put our houses into orbit, telephone, pot-scrubber dishwasher, programmable washing machine and drier, vacuum cleaner, electric tin opener, doors opening and closing, windows up and down, doorbell or knocker, dogs barking, cars going by, sirens, horns, kids' games, people walking and running on the floor above and on the stairs, computer games, cheering for sports events on television, food processors, blenders, electric knives, sanders, water-pick, hair drier, drills and saws, and so much more. And we deal with those things on one level. Cats hear them on other levels, far more acutely. And we must remember that cats can't associate all the sounds they hear with any real value or purpose. Surely any but the dumbest of cats learns to associate the sound of an electric tin opener with a possible food opportunity, but a food processor or a hammer driving a nail are less promising.

It is certain that virtually all of these things have a whole second life at rarefied cycles far above our detection. Cats would hear them there, too. They don't just hear the parts we do. It must be bedlam, and yet cats appear serene most of the time. Either they are more forgiving than we have admitted or they are able to filter sound, as we wondered a little earlier. As they view us, if they are fully tuned in, cats must see a creature that is not only far bigger than is really necessary but far, far noisier than they would consider acceptable except at mating time. No doubt, we are peculiar creatures and vaguely amusing to watch and listen to. I should think we put on something of a freak show, although cats still are comforted by us in many ways. They have found a balance that works for them. It is true we feed them and it is true we imitate their mothers by substituting petting for licking, but considering the level of our social sinning, the things we do right must be awfully important to a cat because I really do not think of cats as being all that tolerant. We are apparently worth the price of admission, oversized and noisy though we may be.

4

Dustbin is a grey and white salvage job. He and his littermates belonged to a couple of drug addicts who had apparently surrendered not only their minds but their souls to their glassine envelopes and white powders. They force-fed all of their pets drugs and kept them in a state of near frenzy from the reports we got. Dustbin was the only survivor, and when he was turned over to us we—our son, actually—forced him to go "cold turkey". It was an act of desperation. We didn't know any other way to do it. It seemed to us he was immensely relieved and today he is even denied access to catmint. He doesn't seem to miss it a bit. He manages to keep himself occupied with the real world of cats and people, and has turned out to be one of the most affectionate cats I have ever known. He simply can't tolerate a vacant lap and makes the most satisfied sounds as soon as he lands and settles down. But he doesn't stay put. Within a minute or two he is up on his feet facing you, forefeet on your chest, butting his face against yours. His target is your chin and cheek near the corner of your mouth. He puts the corner of his mouth in the target zone and with eyes half closed rubs. It is gentle and vaguely pleasing as he rubs again and again and then settles back down on your lap and goes to sleep. Having thus "marked" you, he will sleep as long as you will sit still. He has completed what to him is a very important task.

"Marking" is only one bit of evidence we have of how sensitive a cat's sense of smell really is. Daisy is our oldest continuous resident. She is a tiny cat who is made to look much larger than she actually is by a wonderful fluffy coat. She, too, was a "save". She made it into our fold as an abandoned waif when she was barely able to manage solid food. She was spoon-fed on a complicated menu of soft mashes concocted for her alone. She is in her mid- to late teens now and apparently immortal. She is another cat that shows just how absurd the "independent cat" fiction is. She loves to be held, carried (preferably on her back in a cradle formed between your forearm and torso), and petted. Despite her size, she is the biggest glutton I have ever known. They say you can tell when a cat is going downhill because they go off their feed. Daisy is here forever if her appetite is any kind of a measuring tool.

Daisy is an inveterate marker, too. Her speciality is the leg of the chair where a favourite person is sitting. If you hold her in your lap and pet her vigorously enough, she will mark your face the way Dustbin does, but she seems to prefer your ankle or chair leg, especially if you are at the dining room table. Again, as most cats seem to do, she does her marking in what appears to be a semi-trance, eyes mostly closed, the very softest of satisfied sounds coming from deep down in her throat and spastic little shoves and pushes. Both Dustbin and Daisy like it if you rub the corners of their mouths in the course of a petting session. They reach up and thrust to help you make them happy. Cats can be very co-operative when something feels good which, to a cat, is the way everything is supposed to feel as much of the time as possible. Never underestimate the power of hedonism. It kept more than a few emperors and empresses content for as long as they kept their heads.

What is "marking"? It is not simply rubbing. It is a function of the sense of smell, and it gives our cats yet another avenue into the world around them. We have no real parallel that we can yet identify, but many animals, cats included, produce what are apparently not terribly subtle odours known as pheromones. They are distinctly different chemicals and are part of a communication system. We might think of them as subtle because we are nowhere near acute enough to detect them, but to animals they are wonderfully compelling. The word "pheromone" means, literally, carrying excitation. Dogs have pheromones in their urine, which is why a male dog urinates a few drops at a time after sniffing trees, hydrants, and hubcaps when you take him for a walk. He is leaving messages for other dogs that his territory is staked. Other males come along, of course, and mark the same territory, so what works perfectly well for wolves is mitigated somewhat by the confusion of civilisation. But for a great many animals urinating is a game of one-upmanship. Deer use at least six different kinds of glands to mark territory and challenge or attract other deer. Some primates and fruit bats mark their places on tree limbs; moths have a sex attractant that is stunningly powerful, possibly the most powerful in the world. A minute drop of the come-and-get-it pheromone of a female moth can be detected miles away by a male when it is at a concentration of a few parts in trillions. Those great fluffy antennae on a moth's head are not feelers, as they have been called but chemoreceptors to detect that bewitching sex attractant, whose presence, despite our rather large noses, can't ever be acknowledged by us.

Cats have a very active sense of smell. It is all so far beyond anything we can even approach that it might as well be a sixth sense. There is no doubt, considering where we come from, that we were once a part of that wonderful world of complex odours, but we have traded it off, probably for the almost unbelievable powers of cognition we possess. Why we could not have both the power to reason and a nose that could interpret the world I do not know.

The first sense a kitten has at its disposal is almost certainly smell. Without it, it would have a difficult time locating its own teat, and most kittens do tend to stake out a single nipple for their own use shortly after they are born. That is important in a hunting species. When the usually overworked mother flops down near her kittens or cubs, it is important that everybody get down to business quickly without a lot of useless squabbling and shoving. If each kitten knows just where to go, guided by smell and touch—because, as I said earlier, it all starts before its eyes or ears are available—the mother can get her brood fed and be off hunting again. It is literally a pit stop, and the most important sense that allows every member of the crew to do its job with a minimum of fuss is smell.

What equipment does a cat have for smelling? Its nasal cavities are filled with a series of bony plates called turbinals. They are really baffles

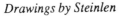

Drawings by Steinlen

whose job it is to greatly increase the surface area where airborne scent particles or molecules can be accumulated for conversion to signals to the brain. A layer of tissue containing astronomical numbers of olfactory cells covers the plates. They are particularly dense toward the rear of the chambers and on the upper covering of the individual turbinals. Despite the small size of a cat's head the number of scent-analysing cells is larger, not relatively larger, but actually larger than in human beings. We have somewhere between 5 and 20 million such cells. A cat has 67 million! Since cats do not trail prey by scent anywhere near to the extent a dog does, cats fall far short of scent hounds. A bloodhound, king of them all, has between 100 and 300 million olfactory cells. But even with a paltry 67 million cells, cats must be treated to a bewildering symphony of smells we can never know exists. As it is with sound detection, cats live where we can never go. Even in our own homes, compared with our cats, we live and are familiar with only a tiny corner of every room.

Cats have a second scenting system wholly independent of their noses. It has the somewhat unpleasant name of vomeronasal organ, or Jacobson's organ. We don't have one so it is a wholly foreign world of sensation for us. Many other animals do have them, however, including species as diverse as bighorn sheep and rattlesnakes. The organ sits far forward in the roof of the cat's mouth. It is not even linked to the same part of the brain where the olfactory nerves go but to two other areas of the hypothalamus, the areas that provide motivation for feeding and the part that triggers complex patterns of sexual behaviour. Obviously those are areas best served or served to best purpose by a chemical awareness of the surrounding world and the opportunities it is offering at the moment.

Many animals lucky enough to be furnished with Jacobson's organ practise a strange ritual. It is called *flehmen*, which is German and for which there is really no translation. When an animal does it, we say it *flehms*. In effect it touches an item or area of interest with its nose and sometimes its tongue. It then raises its head and inhales with its partially open mouth while holding its breath. You can try it but it won't do you any good and you will look awfully silly. Your cat might enjoy watching you try. During the exercise, the typical *flehmer* rolls its upper lip back and wrinkles its nose (rattlesnakes have to skip that bit, they don't have the necessary facial muscles). What is happening is that the rush of air and the tongue are combining to bring a maximum number of scent particles to Jacobson's organ for analysis and relaying to the brain. The nose, in the meantime, has sent its intelligence up and back; when all of the data has been fed in, the brain smells just as it sees and hears, and starts response signals back down the appropriate neuro links: *mount it, eat it, suck, lick, kill, cuddle, split, stay cool,* or *go back to sleep and I'll keep watch with your ears,* or whatever.

The cat can spread pheromones with more than the corners of its mouth. There are glands variously located on the tail, on each side of the

forehead (thus the butting display), they are very abundant there, on the lips and chin, and liberally around the anus. Male cats, of course, spray their urine to place scent marks and establish turf. Pheromones do more than inform, although they come in along the olfactory route and reach the same areas of the brain other smells do as well as via Jacobson's organ. They elicit powerful responses and probably play a very dynamic role in launching cats into mating and mothering, and other patterns both critical and complex. If the pheromones are sexual announcements, then Jacobson's organ may play a more important role than the olfactory chambers in getting the data up to computer central. We aren't sure just what the balance is and whether it shifts according to the situation. Are Jacobson's organ and the regular sense of smell in a cat like the treble and bass response in a hi-fi set? Perhaps the cat is constantly fine-tuning, perhaps that procedure is on autopilot the way our sound filtration is. We don't know if there is any measure of control at all or whether it is in an automatic scanning mode. It is an area that offers a great many research opportunities, many of which can probably be handled by field observation or at least without seriously inconveniencing the study subjects.

Cats apparently recognise each other by smell more than they do by sight. The nose-to-nose ceremony among non-threatening old friends is usually followed by anal sniffing and that causes something of an etiquette problem for cat owners and their pets. A familiar old cat will jump up on your lap (just as Dustbin does), mark you, bump noses, and then turn its back to you and stick its tail straight up in the air and hunch its back. It doesn't take a lot of imagination to figure out what *that* means. That is an invitation, of course, to sniff his anus. Few people, I should imagine, care to recognise the gesture and fewer yet accept the invitation. (Quite frankly, I have never seen the gesture taken up by the human member of the relationship.) But that is just plain rude from the cat's point of view, rather like refusing to shake hands or acknowledge a verbal greeting. It is likely to remain an unresolved problem because we are evolving away from that sort of thing for the most part and it is probably just as well.

Before trying to piece together how we appear to cats in the world of smell, we should mention catmint or catnip, as it is also known, *Nepeta cataria.* (A kind of garden heliotrope—*Leriana officinalis*—and a Japanese weed called matatabi or silver vine—*Actinidia polygama*—seem to act as effectively.) Response to catmint (and presumably the other weeds we have mentioned) is genetically predetermined. Some cats go wild for it and others do not. Only the most susceptible cats cannot be easily distracted. Cats that are really tuned in can detect the volatile oils of catmint when its intensity in the air is on the order of one part per billion.

What all of this adds up to is that cats live in a scent-enriched world and they monitor scent particles with noses that are analogous to our own but very much more refined, as well as that wonderful array known as Jacobson's organ. At least three areas of the brain are on line to receive, sort out, and react to what we collectively call smell, for lack of a better word or an analogous capacity in ourselves. In general, with far less equipment, we do much the same kind of thing but with nowhere near the intensity. We react positively and negatively to perspiration (that certainly must be connected to our sexual patterns and drives), we virtually always eschew any scents connected with elimination and have turned our backs on our primate past and refuse to sniff each other in what have become rude places, at least in public. We are not actively aware of pheromones but we do use surrogates, artificially created scents for which we often pay obscene prices. Used-car salesmen spray new car smells to subliminally tempt buyers and we burn absurdly expensive candles with French names to get the onion, fish and yes, the cat smells out of our houses, or at least bury them in a layer of often cloying replacement odours.

Drawing by Steinlen

There are surely smells cats don't like (but that is not when they curl their lips, remember, they *flehm* when they love a smell), but not too many of these odours are related directly to us as creatures. They butt us and bump noses with us and generally offer us all manner of social opportunities, whether or not we have showered after exerting ourselves, whether we are wearing cologne, perfume, or after-shave lotion and whether or not we are wearing clean socks. They take us as we are. Yet they do smell us very clearly. Interestingly enough, while as individual creatures in their ken we are much larger than would probably make sense to them, and far noisier than would seem polite to them in anything but the mating mode, we probably are far less stimulating to their noses. We are surrounded by, or at least we surround ourselves with wonderful smells, the simmering pot of clam chowder on the stove, but as sweating and otherwise exuding animals we are probably dull as the water we use to wash the chowder pot. Since we are not objects of sexual interest, the cat's Jacobson's organ probably pretty much ignores us, especially since we are essentially inedible. We probably do absolutely nothing to the areas of the feline hypothalamus connected with those functions.

As we attempt to unravel and clarify the ways cats may picture us we have to isolate or at least attempt to isolate their individual senses. But no cat ever has a uni-sense picture of anything as complex as a human being, any more than we can lift a cat out of context and evaluate it with one of our senses only. We are a composite in the cat's mind and we must not ignore that fact. Coming in through even the four channels we have examined so far (the two forms of smell, hearing, and seeing), we must be a monstrous intrusion on what might otherwise be a harmonious world. Still, cats obviously like us, and they certainly think we are interesting or quaint or something signal for they continue to watch us after an association that can be reckoned in the thousands of years.

5

W e are down, now, to the last two feline senses of which we can speak with any degree of certainty. We are soon going to be far less surefooted as we attempt to enter the world of the cat and look back to see ourselves. The two remaining certain senses are taste and touch. We will go to touch first because it is the keener of the two and certainly the more important to the cat as it attempts to understand us.

Touch, as we indicated earlier, is very close to hearing. Almost certainly they both came down to the modern cats from a common origin in animals far more primitive than mammals. Hearing is a reaction to vibration in an elastic medium. Rating them qualitatively, airborne vibrations are not that much different from vibrations that come at a hearing organism through the air or through a liquid which in almost all imaginable cases would be water. It is possible to imagine a single complex set of vibrations coming all three ways simultaneously. As far-fetched as it may seem, imagine a cat swimming in very shallow water during an earthquake. Not the image of an everyday feline experience but it makes the point.

A vibration is a rapidly, almost relentlessly repeated touch. It is quite possible that a cat "hears" in the broader sense, with particularly sensitive areas of skin like the soles or pads of its paws, even when the happening is far short of our hypothetical earth tremor, something as light and delicate as a mouse thundering by. Where does actual hearing leave off and touch take over? Since they are so reinforcing of each other the distinction is not always easy to make and may in fact be best viewed as a continuum impacting on different areas of sensitivity.

Before leaving our earthquake behind we should acknowledge that many animals, cats apparently among them, are far more sensitive to things like changes in the earth than we are. It is not easy to catalogue the senses involved or know to what extent each is used, but any action in the substratum gets to animals, cat included, long before we see pictures go crooked on the wall and dishes start to clatter to the floor. There have been times when animals from cockroaches to chipmunks have been seen acting tense and to some degree disorientated days before there was any human awareness of impending disaster. There is potentially very meaningful research on this happening right now in China and California, among other places.

Feline skin is very sensitive to touch but surprisingly insensitive to temperature changes. That is ironic when we consider how hedonistic cats are. We think of them as seeking optimum experiences in all things,

including temperature. We humans start to feel pain when anything we pick up or allow to come to rest against our skin passes 112 degrees Fahrenheit. A cat won't even begin to feel uncomfortable until that temperature reaches 124 degrees. If we humans did not have the rudimentary sense of smell we work with, our fluffy little Daisy would possibly never know she had her tail in the fire when she sits on the hearth. It has happened often. Fortunately, burning cat hair really smells awful.

Millions of cats every year are saved from harm because there are people around to shoo them off the stove, away from the fireplace and other sources of significantly high temperature. These episodes are usually accompanied by remarks about "stupid cat" and "idiot", yet it isn't intellectual acuity or the lack thereof that makes cats relatively insensitive to heat but rather the design and distribution of nerve endings and sensory cells. Puzzle: Nature in her wisdom has evolved her cats to be somewhat insensitive to hot and cold, but why has she made them indifferent to the smell of their own hind ends when they are about to go up in flames? It is not a subtle smell. It is not one a cat could possibly miss, but it is one cats blissfully ignore presumably until the last minute. We don't know about that for certain because we never let it get that far. How far would it have to go before the cat said *phew* or *ouch*? Of course, the original cat was not designed (read *evolved*) with fire in mind.

The cat's relative insensitivity to temperature does not hold for the nose pad or the area immediately around it on the animal's snout. Quite to the contrary. The cat's upper lip is extremely sensitive to temperature and can detect a change up or down of little more than one degree, perhaps less. The reason for that or at least an early use of that capacity is kitten feeding. Between touch (including touching "temperature") and smell, the first two of the kitten's senses to come on line, and all of that within minutes of birth, the helpless little thing can find a teat and nurse. It may be destined to be blind and deaf for ten days or even two weeks, but the little glutton can smell and heat-seek its way to survival. It is absolutely essential that that be so. It is one of those exquisite little things that cats like all animals have built in during their evolution upward towards unknown species goals.

The hairs in a cat's pelt, including the whiskers, which we will come back to shortly, are really nothing more than extensions of the creature's skin. That skin includes an enormous number of "touch spots", areas that are more sensitive than the skin immediately around them. They may be as densely packed as anywhere between seven and twenty-seven to the square centimetre of skin. The cat's skin generally is quite remarkable in design. On the back of the neck it is at least five times as thick as the skin on the back of the hind legs. It is loose and "flowing", which suggests that cats, predators though they may be, have often been prey as well. Loose skin makes squirming out of an enemy's clutches much easier no matter how the cat is grabbed. Cats also are able to work their way through difficult passageways because loose-skinned animals are far less likely to get hung up than tight-skinned animals. One thing appears certain: cats are always fully aware of anything touching them and certainly anything attempting to restrain them. The fur, as we will see, does not have to be actually touched by an object. The air flow rebounding from a solid object can be enough to put a cat on alert. The skin is an organ of touch even when it is being touched second hand, and that probably is more true of that part of the skin known as coat.

The most complex part of a cat's pelt are the greatly enlarged, enormously stiffened hairs we call whiskers. Vibrissae is their proper name, and they grow on the upper lip, to some extent over the eyes, far back on the cheeks, and even on the backs of the forelegs. The odd placement of the leg vibrissae probably has something to do with the fact that cats frequently hug or grasp their prey. That, however, is supposition, albeit a reasonably informed guess. Many whiskered animals also have vibrissae under their chins. Cats do not because they don't muzzle around in the dirt or on a trail while hunting. They don't need extra touch sensitivity there so it has pretty much evolved away. Surely cats are descended from animals that had many more of them there.

The whiskers on the upper lip are arranged in four rows that extend well beyond the width of a cat's head. They can be fanned out on command and are verifiers, particularly when light is low. They supplement sight. They judge which openings a cat's body will clear, they feel around for food that is too close for the eyes or nose to focus on. (That is not the same thing as chin whiskers in another species being worked through leaves and ground debris. It is not a contradiction but a matter of style. Cats don't root, if you please. Rooting is just not them.)

The whiskers or vibrissae are at least twice as thick as ordinary cat hairs

and are imbedded at least three times as deeply in the skin. At their bulbous ends deep down inside the dermal layers, there are masses of nerve endings that can receive and transmit information about touch and even information about changes in air pressure, which is touch in the final analysis. There are, on the average in a normally configurated cat, twenty-four whiskers. The top two rows can move independently of the bottom two. Apparently rows two and three are the most sensitive and useful rows of all.

In their various locales, the vibrissae grow either singly or in tufts. They can act like levers and pivot, translating the slightest contact to the sensory cells at their roots. As with all of the cat's senses, those data are passed along to the brain, which feels and reacts just as it sees and reacts, hears and reacts, and smells and tastes and reacts. It all has to go to central control. The cat's mainframe processes all incoming information and generally combines the data from all the sources at the same time and puts them into a single context. It is that context that starts the flow of reactions and instructions out along the network to the animal's muscles. We must remember the cat doesn't have to wait very long for instructions. It is all virtually instantaneous and probably just about all reflexive, that is, the cat doesn't have to think about shooting a paw out to nail a mouse crossing its field of vision. The primitive parts of the cat's brain tell the paw what to do, not any cognition centre the cat might have. It is not really any different from our touching something hot. Our hand pulls back long before we have time to cogitate. If we took time to say, "Oh my, my nerve endings have informed my brain that this thing is burning me badly and my brain says I should do something about that fact. I think I shall withdraw my hand to a safer place," we would long ago have sizzled away. It is left to the spinal cord to supply first stop-gap responses in matters of dire emergency. In pretty much if not exactly the same way, a cat does not have time to discuss a scurrying mouse with itself or the mouse would become a vague memory well before the cat could begin to raise its paw.

The most impressive thing about a cat's whiskers, probably, is that they don't have to come into contact with solid objects to feed data to the mainframe. It is likely that tiny vibrations feed them information, and air currents careening off solids like a sound echo off a canyon wall feed the same system by deflection. That could explain why cats seldom if ever bump into things. Rarely is it too dark for them to see at least the shape and size of an obstacle, and it never can be dark enough to keep air currents from flowing against and rebounding from possible hazards. At least the vibrissae part of their coat can read those currents as a magnet can a bar of iron. Perhaps that is what people mean when they suggest that cats can see without any light. They can't really see but they can sense.

Here again we see how impossible it is to compartmentalise sensation. All of the senses are co-operative. Vibrations within the hearing range are taken in for processing by the ears, are felt by the feet and perhaps by various parts of a cat's fur, especially those long, stiff parts known as vibrissae. Where eyes and nose can't focus, those same vibrissae do the job and also verify what the cat can see. These overlaps, verifications, and duplicated interpretations, all going to the same interpretive centre, come close to constituting whole new sensory packages. They come close to transcending that old, universally accepted number of five.

But what of touch in the cat and the measure of man? To a cat, we are probably not much more than a big obstacle much of the time. Cats don't bump into us unless they want a good bit of rubbing or they want to stake a claim on our ankles or our dining room chair. As for vibrissae contact, it probably depends on how the individual cat feels about us. If I catch Omari (and don't get clawed to ribbons) and touch his whiskers, the signal in the brain is surely, *To arms, to arms, Alarm, alarm.* On the other hand, if Squid, Xnard, or Daisy jumps up into my lap for a little interaction time and I touch their whiskers, they screw up their faces, squint an eye or two almost closed, and seem to be hearing *Ah nice, Ah, nice* from central control. The same physical sensation is surely coloured by attitude and past relationships. Generally speaking no cat likes too much contact with its whiskers, like playful tugging, probably because it cuts them off from or at least clutters up a major source of information. It would be somewhat like shouting in their ear or repeatedly flashing a powerful light directly into their eyes.

We did have a strange anomaly in our animal family, however. Kate, our loving lynx-point Siamese who has gone on ahead, liked to chew whiskers. The other cats, for reasons I have never been able to fathom, would sit like dummies and allow Kate to gnaw their all-important vibrissae down to stubs. They looked silly while it was going on and sillier yet when it was over. She did it to sleeping dogs, too. I know of no parallel to this barbering instinct among wild felids or canids and have no explanation. It would have seemed to be anywhere from useless to detrimental to the barbereds although it obviously satisfied some slightly misplaced social grooming instinct in Kate.

That is one thing about cats; no sooner do you think you know it all when you are sharply arrested in your silly reverie and sent limping back to square one. I have never known a cat that couldn't do that to you. It is a strange form of perversity. Perhaps putting us in our places is an imperative with cats that we also don't yet understand. What sense or senses are involved is difficult to say, yet it is in the very nature of the beast

to ridicule our so-called superior intellects. *"Have us down pat, do you? Try this one on for size."*

Touch is important in the man-cat relationship because we do pat our companions to express our feelings for them and to tranquillise ourselves when our own nerves are frazzled by the world around us. It is interesting to note how different cats like different forms of petting. With many cats to touch their stomach is to bleed, while other cats appear to love it. In fact a cat on its back with its tender undersides exposed is terribly vulnerable to attack and most cats take exception to that measure of liberty on our part. For a cat to allow its stomach to be scratched is for it to show enormous trust and affection. Some cats like their petting to be fairly vigorous, others insist on the very softest touches only. Some like you to rub the glands near their mouths, others seem to want to reserve that touch for themselves. Some cats like it if you make a ring of your thumb and forefinger and clamp fairly tightly on their tails and slide along it. Others hate having their tails touched at all. Our enchanting silver ash tabby Siafu (that is Swahili for "little biting ant", his sister's name is Safari or "journey", and their mother's is Maridadi, which is Swahili for "beautiful") has a weird touch pattern that he loves. It requires the human participant to sit on the floor, roll Siafu onto his back, grab him by the middle, and shove him across the rough-textured floor tiles to someone who is waiting to catch him and shoot him back the same way. He loves being used as a bowling ball, without the ten pins, of course. I think it is more the fact that he is being invited to interact than anything else that brings him pleasure.

6

The fifth and last conventional sense is taste. Actually, if you consider smell in combination with the Jacobson's organ, where the animal properly equipped can *taste* the air as one and a half or even two senses, conventional taste would be the fifth-and-a-half or sixth. However, palatability is a combination of touch, smell, and taste. Touch provides information about texture, smell gives the animal's central control a chemical analysis of floating particles that break loose from the potential food substances and float or can be drawn upward by a current of air. In contrast, actual taste, the kind we experience, is the chemical analysis of particles that are carried to the sensitive cells by saliva. The salivary glands secrete enzymes which break down organic material so that the taste buds can respond to their chemical properties. That information, coupled with texture and smell data, comes together in the brain and is interpreted as good food, bad food, or not food at all. The taste buds are most dense towards the back of the tongue. Thousands of nerve cells in clusters work as chemical *feelers* and generally keep the cat from eating things that are bad for it. That doesn't work 100 per cent of the time, unfortunately. An unknown number of cats die from ingested poisons every year. We have lost at least one cat to a philodendron plant someone brought as a house gift. We had every intention of taking it out to the dustbin as soon as our guests left, but a young and inexperienced cat got into it while we were eating dinner. A few leaves was all that it took. I am not sure that experience was a factor. I have heard of adult cats dying from the same cause. It is apparently a lesson that a cat can't learn without putting its life on the line.

The taste buds have at least five *modalities*: sweet, sour, salt, bitter, and water. Those five analytical groupings working in co-operation and supplemented by information about airborne particles, or smell, plus texture give the cat's brain all the data it needs. It is a very sophisticated system, but it does fall down when information about what is good and what is bad is not on line for reference. It is exactly like the word processor on which this book is being written. It is complex when compared to a typewriter (actually it is a simple device), but it is hopeless, a great big useless space taker, unless programs are fed into it and electronic glitches or viruses are kept out. The cat, like this machine, has its own RAM (random access memory), some minimal information built in; in the case of a brain, that means genetically acquired; in the case of this machine, memory that is volatile and must be transferred onto a disc or be lost.

An example of genetic *knowledge* is the taste-bud modality for sweetness. Sweet things are far less attractive to cats than they are to other animals, dogs and horses, for example, and bears and elephants. The cat has far fewer taste buds responsive to the sugars than other tastes, and when news of sweetness is relayed to the brain the central control tells the cat to avoid the food. The water-sensitive cells tend to suppress those sugar-sensitive cells that do exist and keep cats from going for the food sending sweet signals. The reason for these safeguards is simple. Sugar is not good for cats in any quantity. It is unfortunate but we have introduced hundreds of new plants from all over the world and tens of thousands of chemicals that we fabricate into our environment and therefore the cat's. Unlike the warning against naturally occurring sugars, the cat does not carry information either in its structure (fewer sensitive taste buds) or its genetic memory for avoidance. Cats can and do get into a great deal of trouble because so much of what we have made available to them is deadly. Hence the wisdom in the proverb, "Curiosity killed the cat".

None of this is to suggest that the cat is a little furry machine that always responds the same way to its environment. They are individuals and have both fixed preferences and moods. If they are bored, they are apt to try something one day that they avoided or at least ignored the day before. With the exception of their extra interpretive power via Jacobson's organ, their method of sampling and savouring food is not materially different from our own and they are just as individualistic. I have known cats to eat chives growing in a pot on the kitchen windowsill. I have known some that adored cantaloupe (despite its sugar content) and

Drawing by Steinlen

others that munched on asparagus and some that liked tomatoes. Texture can be very attractive, apparently. We had a Siamese named Thai Lin that was like a giant moth from a Japanese science-fiction film. In fact we frequently referred to her as Mothra. She loved to eat wool and a number of synthetic fabrics as well. I doubt that she needed such offbeat nourishment. She once ate her way right through an electric blanket and apparently came and went through the opening until we discovered it under a top sheet. We had her at the time crinoline petticoats were back in fashion. More than one guest got a funny look on her face as Thai Lin sat contentedly between her feet munching away on her underskirt. In the case of a long evening skirt a *crunch-crunch* sound was likely to be the first clue we got that the mad petticoat-eater was in the room. It was very difficult to explain to a guest with a newly air-conditioned wardrobe.

Although cats will kill deer mice, they will seldom eat them. They simply don't like the taste. The essence of being a cat, after all, is being selective, since selectivity is the first ingredient in being both hedonistic and materialistic. If you can't be a picky snob there is not much point in being a cat.

House mice, on the other hand, are apparently very savoury. Cats hunt but seldom eat shrews and moles, snakes, frogs, and toads, for the same reason. They move nicely and make great game even if they don't make suitable table fare. Many frogs and toads are poisonous, some far more so than others, or at least have patches of skin that are. Cats spit them out as soon as they pick them up. It is only a fraction of a second between the time a cat's saliva touches that skin and the brain sends a danger signal back down. Frogs and toads also have a texture that is peculiar to amphibians and it is quite possible that that, too, alerts central control.

It has been estimated that the average cat in an average situation sends about ten thousand signals a second to its brain. That number increases if the edge of its peripheral vision is stimulated by a mouse or a ball of wool on the end of a string, by food put in front of it, or by sudden unidentified sounds. The cat's brain, according to some researchers, probably can't handle more than seven to ten signals a second, so do the rest go to waste? There is no facility for storage and recall of signals. If signals could be recalled they would be useless unless fed back in the same sequence they were received. After all, what good could thousands upon thousands of signals all coming forward in a jumble do any animal? Information, like response, does not work when it is random. Since the signals would keep coming at the same minimal rate, at least, the cat would fall hopelessly behind—in one hour it would have 35,640,000 unused signals to contend with. If anything exciting happened in that hour, the number would soar. Still, the brain can process enough information to keep most cats on track most of the time. The brain that doesn't do precisely that is soon starved of oxygen, for its host and all of its other parts are dead.

As far as we have gone down the list of the conventionally acknowledged senses of the cat, the cat is in good shape. The mere fact that a cat exists many minutes beyond birth is proof enough. If touch and smell did not come on line immediately, the kitten could not feed. If hearing and sight didn't switch on at the age of two weeks or less, the kitten would be in jeopardy because its littermates and mother would soon outdistance it, which means the mother would have to set it aside and probably not let it feed at all. No mother cat can long survive herself saddled with a rapidly growing youngster that won't be able to care for itself when it matures. In nature it is the proven breeder, not its babies, that has to live for the species to survive.

A cat's five (or five-and-a-half) senses come built in and are programmed to provide an endless stream of data to a central clearing house, each from a predetermined point after birth. That stream seems like overkill—the brain processing fewer than ten out of ten thousand pieces of information—but it is highly likely that some form of scanning takes place. If that is not so and it is a matter of spot-checking, it must have been worked out a very long time ago that in the kind of life a cat lives, sampling is enough. A third possibility is that there may be a kind of

alarm system that brings the brain's interpretive power into quick focus. The house in which I am sitting has six different alarm systems that can be instantly focused by a signal. If the temperature rises too rapidly, an alarm goes off giving a warning of probable flames. The attic and some other areas have a maximum temperature allowance before signalling a probable problem and there are smoke detectors as well. If doors are opened after the alarm has been engaged, it again signals, and if anything moves in certain selected rooms (which means cats are locked out when the system is on), the police receive notification. The sixth signal tells of a power failure or an effort to monkey with the system. That kind of thing could go on in a cat's brain with the senses substituting for our alarm system's peculiar sensitive areas. Whatever its secrets may be, clearly the cat's interlocking network of sensory apparatus works, for we still have our cats with us and the cats in the wild are wonderfully efficient and would probably continue their course forever if we would only leave them alone.

7

Some people have suggested that balance is a sense, but although it is critical to a cat's survival I am not certain it should be classified in that way. A sense, as I interpret it, alerts a cat to changes in its environment that should be dealt with to the cat's advantage. Why should a cat be alerted to the movements of non-edible animals like hopping frogs and toads? Because it is to the cat's advantage to kill them for practice, and besides, a cat can always make choices once it has been alerted. A cat that has not heard the buzzer might sleep through many needed meals. All living things of small-enough size (that is, relative to the cat's size, however; a zebra, even a baby zebra, while important to a lion, is of little concern to our pillow denter) are educational toys. A cat killing a mole or a shrew is getting ready for the next tasty mouse that can be important prey. I don't think balance alerts a cat to changes in the environment so much as it guides a cat in making its way through the world in which it lives. Perhaps that is more a matter of semantics than anything else, but I hesitate to call balance a sense in the same way we call smell and sight senses. That balance, of course, is a function of a combined system born of cerebellum and vestibular—brain and middle-ear— functions.

It has also been suggested that the judging of temperature is a true sense in cats. Certainly nerve endings in our skin alert us to dangerously high or low temperatures just as other nerves nearby tell us we are being touched for good or bad. All of this is also true of the cat, but it takes more heat to alert them as we have pointed out. In some animals, temperature is a true sense. The best example is found in a group of snakes called the pit vipers. The group includes a number of common American species—all sixty-six of the rattlesnakes, the copperheads, and cottonmouth water moccasins

—and both tropical American and Asian species. All pit vipers are venomous. On each cheek there is a single pit roughly halfway between the eye and the nostril. The pit, open to the outside, is divided into two chambers that are separated by a thin and highly sensitive membrane. Up to a distance of a foot or so, the snake is able to judge the movement of prey by the temperature differential. A mouse whose body temperature is generally higher than the air surrounding it will reveal its left-to-right or right-to-left movement as it shifts its head emanations like a little furnace on legs. It also alerts the snake by coming towards it, straight on or more to one side or the other. If it moves away before the snake strikes, the snake engages Jacobson's organ (it just pays more attention to it, really, since the organ is never switched off) and slithers forward into a better striking position. That, to me, is temperature as a sense in the real meaning of the word "sense". Cats have nothing like that super-refined sensitivity, as far as we know.

In thinking of the cat's brain processing all this data, or as much data as it can handle, far less than comes in, we should keep in mind that a cat's brain and our own are very much alike. We do have the neocortex, the last part of the mammalian brain to evolve. The cat does not have those two big lobes, which are essentially for our speech centre and memory associations, but the rest of the more primitive parts beneath and behind those lobes are virtually identical in our two species. That has been unfortunate for the cat because cats have been used more than any other animal for neurological studies and experiments. It has been stated as unequivocal fact that brain surgery on man today is possible because of work done on cats. That is not pleasing to contemplate, but it is almost assuredly true.

When we look at a schematic drawing of the cat's brain, we are struck by the fact that the sensory evaluation areas are all over the place. The areas for vision and smell are at about opposite sides of the structure, with hearing somewhere in the middle. Touch is off on its own, too. What happens when a mouse moves into view? Those ten thousand or so signals go roaring up their nerve channels and all go squirting into the brain almost at exactly the same time. The brain is not going to take vision's data alone and pass judgement on what is going on out there. Smell makes its report, sound its, and although taste and touch are not needed at once, they are on standby and are no doubt clattering away. Chemicals are

generating electrical impulses and connection points for them—and all of this is happening at an unimaginable speed. The brain somehow is scanning all of the centres, asking the question, one imagines, What have you got for me? The scanning hits all of the centres, selecting perhaps one out of a thousand bits of data, then shuffles the pack. Chemistry and energy again switch back and forth as instructions go back down and out through a response network and appropriate actions are taken. All of this has happened before a mouse can take a step.

The mouse, too, has a mammalian brain and the same battery of basic senses. Is the cat's paw quicker than the mouse's feet? Probably not. The cat's nervous system and large brain probably give it a shorter response time. Our domestic cat's brain is closer in proportionate size and general performance to its wild ancestors' than that of any other domestic animal. Our pigs, although they can be mean devils when they return to the wild (go feral), have brains and personalities far removed from those of their fierce wild boar antecedents. The same is true of the horse, our cattle, and even the dog. A dog's brain is one third smaller as measured against body weight than its ancestor's, the wolf's. Domestic cats, when they get the right stimulation, behave almost exactly as wild cats would, and no cat watcher has ever failed to make note of that. As of this writing I have been on twenty-one African safaris and about a dozen Asian *shikar*. I have seen a lot of wildcats both large and small. Many I have watched for hours, and try as I will to keep my observations pure, I see the house cat in the wildcat, even in lions weighing over four hundred pounds. It is a comparison that is unavoidable because it is valid.

A cat pouncing on a mouse is not really very different from you swatting a mosquito. It works the same way because the important area of the brain for mouse pouncing and mosquito murder are so close in our two species. In fact, it is very often involuntary, or just about so, in us. Example? I had an ambition that stayed with me for years. I am a great admirer of elephants and I have watched thousands of them in the wild in both Africa and Asia. For some reason I had always wanted to walk among them and neither disturb them nor, I hoped, be disturbed by them. I knew it was possible with elephants that were not being hunted and had been used to man in relatively close proximity. I was with an elephant researcher who had spent years watching a particular herd and he confessed that he had had the same ambition and had realised it. I did some very serious fussing and he agreed to take me through an area near a marsh where the elephants were used to seeing him as he sat with his binoculars and took his notes. I promised I would never tell on him, and at a propitious time with no other humans in sight we started off, slowly.

At a distance of twenty feet, several of the elephants turned to watch us. They spread their ears not in alarm and not really as a threat but to monitor our sounds carefully and perhaps to increase their size and remind us of what we were dealing with, as if that was necessary! No one had to tell me that I was to walk in a straight line behind the researcher, who was familiar to the animals, and not talk. No one had to tell me to keep my speed constant and to avoid any sudden moves. It was absolutely essential to keep from alarming the animals.

Then it happened. A tse-tse fly landed on my cheek. I know from long experience just how much a tse-tse bite hurts and on this occasion without thinking, without engaging in anything I could later call a voluntary action, I swatted at the fly. I missed the fly, smacked myself in the face with a loud noise, and thoroughly alarmed twenty-three elephants with the sudden movement and the unexpected sound. As elephants spun in place (and they can do that with stunning agility), they really spread their ears, and a few of them thrust out their trunks for a better smell; we slowed our pace but kept moving in a straight line. Luckily none of the elephants kicked up dust with a forefoot (that is an ominous gesture) or pulled down vegetation and tossed it in the air. Only one, a young male feeling his oats, made a little mock charge. We moved on out of the herd and when we were clear we said in unison, "That was stupid." And it had been, but it had also been done not only without thinking but without plan. It was an automatic response, the kind cats must make by the score every day.

That is the kind of brain we both have. When a mouse runs into a cat's field of peripheral vision and all that chemistry and electricity spins up

Drawing by Steinlen

and down the channels, there simply can be no time to think. Our brains, in order to contend with predictable recurring episodes, have evolved a gear ratio so high it works without our interference. Men do not usually walk through herds of elephants. I had introduced an unexpected element into the elephants' lives and my own. Men do have to keep the number of mosquito and tse-tse fly bites they get to as few as possible, however, given malaria and the dreadful diseases the tse-tse fly carries. It is more important for the brain to work quickly enough to eliminate biting insects than it is to respect territoriality or at least *space* among elephants. It is a certainty that every progenitor from whom I inherited genetic material swatted both flies and mosquitoes.

Could I have overriden my reflexive action while strolling among the elephants? Almost certainly had I not been so involved with the thrill of the moment. I was feeling, not thinking. And that is probably much the same with cats. They jump a mouse just about every time they see one but will certainly stop if a Rottweiler or Doberman Pinscher is about to attack the same target. It all happens quicker than quick in both man and cat. There are checks, though, when both of our species are able to switch to thinking instead of reacting, and thereby interefere with the automatic mode of responding. In a very real sense it is a matter of our butting into our own lives.

8

Cats do have ways of judging time, not as time elapsed, I am certain, but as time arrived. I doubt if any cat ever had the means of telling that three hours, three days, or even three weeks have elapsed since such-and-such happened, but they certainly have ways of knowing from their own body's signals that the time has come to raise Cain over there being no food in the dish. You don't need a clock to tell you that you are hungry and neither does a cat. That is one reason why I have never been able to accept time judgement as an actual sense independent of other stimulation, but some people still claim it is just that.

Signals not only come from inside man and cat alike but there are all kinds of interesting things that happen outside that could help a cat stay on schedule. In many areas, winds come up at a certain time of the day and may whistle through trees and shrubs or even through architectural details on a building. They could be at frequencies we don't hear, but that would be like clarion calls to any animal with hearing as acute as that of a cat. Little wonder that a cat without a quartz watch on its paw that arrives at the same place each day is a little spooky to some people, but it can be explained quite easily in any number of ways. Just as sounds come, often on schedule, they go. In some areas, the winds die down at the same time each day, and a world without wind doesn't sound like one with the air in motion, colliding, shrilling, reverberating, and even thundering. Then there are *photo* signals. The length of time there is light of a certain density varies day by day on a regular swing dependably one year long. There are seasonal signals often too numerous to count. Smells certainly change as spring bulbs erupt from earth newly thawed; certain flowers, some so minute we would hardly notice them, bloom according to their own schedule, and then, of course, right on schedule leaves fall. Even when we don't burn them, they have a certain unmistakable smell that changes as the hours and the days pass. The plant world is cycling to or away from high points every hour of every day, and each step in each sequence, every event, has a different smell that could signal time past and time approaching to any animal with a good sense of smell. We have not the foggiest notion how cats pick up on signals or where they plug into things we can't join in the enjoyment of. But it is entirely possible for a cat to come to associate an event with an odour and amaze us by pre-responding to an event it knows is coming, perhaps not consciously, but unconscious knowledge is still knowledge that can help guide any creature through the movement of the hours or the seasons.

Some of the most reliable signals come quite naturally from other animals. Birds sing in a special way at nest-building and mate-seeking time. They are territorial and combative and it is ironic that that is when their songs are sweetest. However we may interpret them aesthetically, they are distinctly season-related. Cats almost certainly don't get very deeply involved in aesthetics but they do pick up guiding signals. Baby birds in their nests peep out their impatient calls for food and migrating birds far overhead, even or perhaps especially on overcast days, send volumes of sound and seasonal data tumbling earthwards. Mosquitoes and other man-eating insects move according to a shared time schedule. They don't compete because they emerge and hunt and feed at different times of the day and night, and they all have their peculiar hums and buzzes. One mosquito may sound like all mosquitoes to us, but it would be foolish to assume any such insensitivity for cats. Crickets sound off, and so do bats, and so do frogs and toads. The world around us is a symphony of sound, but we get only a bit of it. In fact, the sum total of our sensory experience is little more than the tip of that proverbial iceberg. Cats get most if not all of it and are probably therefore much more attentive than we are. I don't find very much that is mysterious in the fact that cats, bombarded from within and without, manage to appear or disappear or do anything else on what appears to be a timed schedule. The very concept of a schedule is human. Cats don't think of things as being scheduled, they simply respond appropriately. That is exactly what they are doing almost assuredly without any awareness of elapsed time. When the old fire horse heard the bells, he didn't look at the big clock on the wall, but he did back into the traces on the engine he knew he would be

called upon to pull careening over the cobblestone streets to the scene of a fire. When he smelled the fire, he moved even faster and pulled even harder. So do cats, in their own way. Time actually is an event for a cat, not a sequence, and too many people, I think, make rather too much of that fact. There is so much that is amazing about a cat, we don't have to be creative or stretch points to appreciate them for what they are.

Another bit of cat lore that has cats doing things they probably don't really do centres on that old bogey called precognition, the subject that Professor I. J. Good used to mystify me. The anecdotes one hears usually centre on people being about to take a trip or people expecting company. The story typically has someone about to go to Europe or some other distant place for business or a holiday and the cat making life miserable for them for hours or days in advance. There are variations on the theme, of course. Many stories have women about to leave for the hospital to have children, or kids about to leave for camp. Cats use open, half-packed suitcases for littertrays (an exceedingly unpleasant habit but very graphic), steal balled-up socks, spray, mess in the corner, refuse to eat, hide, scratch, sulk, whimper, and vocalise in many eerie ways not typical of them on a good day. They get out and run away, show signs of being in heat even though they are spayed, show signs of sexual anxiety even though they are altered, fight with other animals, demand an inordinate amount of attention, or engage in some or all of the above. We have on the one hand the fact that people are indeed planning to move, travel, or have babies, and on the other the undeniable fact that a cat is making a first-class pest of himself. Ergo, there is ESP. Not really, at least not necessarily. We must not forget that the premise of this book, in fact its title, is *A Cat Is Watching*.

Cats are extremely sensitive to their human family. Indifference, or the appearance of indifference, is a ploy. It is a game cats play or, perhaps, the way cats play the game. We are rhythmic creatures—all animals are—and the rhythms that make us hum are easy for an observant animal to pick up on. They are also what makes them secure. That is what the preceding discussion of how the cat's senses work was all about. By engaging those senses and honing in on us, cats have our rhythms down cold, and fortunately for our cats we each have different rhythms they can go by. Changes in schedule, activity, or even attitude are likely to be anything from worrisome to downright disturbing to the cat in residence. Cats hate change, in most instances, because cats rely on internal and externally generated signals to reassure them that all is well with their world, i.e., they are still in control. Water is where it should be, food becomes available when it should, the sun shines through a certain window at a certain time, and there are pillows or a piano or a spot on the rug that can be relied upon to be warm for napping. Outdoor cats know when the mice run and where to set up the ambush, and a bird singing in a tree in a certain way tells the hunter to watch a special hole because it won't be long before the baby chipmunks appear there. But then there is suddenly the spectre of change, hated change. We give off signals that foretell our intentions to change the cat's orderly world, and all of this without permission, if you please. Why shouldn't a cat use an open, half-packed suitcase for a litter tray? The last five times he saw that device in that condition, you went away and threw his world all awry. An unwelcome house/pet sitter began coming and never offered play or treats. Your cat is enough of a people watcher to get angry when he sees the suitcase first come out of the attic or from the under the bed or off the shelf in the wardrobe. It is bad news.

Naturally, he steals socks. You put things in, he takes things out. Maybe he can get you to change your mind. At the very least he can tell you how he feels about things.

Anyone who doubts that women and their husbands act differently as the time for their child's birth approaches hasn't been much of a people watcher. The woman moves differently, smells differently almost certainly, and new paraphernalia starts arriving. The cat inspects it all as he would inspect anything new or different that comes into his world, but cannot for the life of him see any use for a crib, stroller, high chair, bassinet, or a mobile consisting of tasteless plastic or rubber ducks. A room gets repapered and repainted, new curtains go up, good old reliable furniture gets shoved off, put away, or just disappears. No people-watching cat could fail to pick up on all of those strange and for the moment meaningless signals. Something is up and the cat is not in on it. So why not spray the curtains and send a signal that enough is enough? Either show why all of this is being done or stop it. That is what the cat is saying.

It is certain that as long as people look back at their cats, there will be enchanting anecdotes about extrasensory perception. In fact I do believe very firmly that cats have senses beyond the big five-and-a-half but I don't think that what they do in half-packed suitcases tells us what we need to know. We have to look well beyond that kind of very obvious act. What are the things cats do that are not readily explained by their use of the typical mammalian sensory complex?

9

The story is told of a family moving from Portland, Oregon, to the Los Angeles area. After the van had left with all of their wordly possessions, the family climbed into their estate car, mother, father, three kids, and a dog and a cat, and headed for their new life in Southern California. Well along in the trip, just south of Santa Barbara, they stopped for a picnic lunch and when no one was looking the cat, a ten-year-old altered Siamese male, vanished. There was deep grass and plenty of undergrowth nearby and there were a million places where the cat could have been hiding or have got into trouble. After securing their dog, the family set out and literally beat the bushes. No luck. They tramped and called and pleaded until dusk, then checked into a nearby motel. At sun-up they were out again with dishes of food and the same pleading tone in their voices. At noon they broke off the search, reported their loss to the local veterinary hospital and the police in the nearest town, and called every humane society they could locate for miles around. Their life was complicated by the fact that they didn't have their new phone number, but they made a deal with the veterinary surgeon to hold the cat for them if it was turned in. Then they continued their trip south. After several fruitless calls to the vet they accepted the fact that their cat was gone. And as any pet owner can tell you, that is the worst feeling of all, not knowing. It is almost better to find a body than never know what became of your pet.

But six months later, the wife's sister phoned. The cat had turned up in their old neighbourhood in Portland and had been taken in by former neighbours. It appeared to be a little worse for wear but it was alive and reasonably healthy. Eventually it was shipped south and settled into a quiet life in a suburb of Los Angeles. It never strayed again.

Questions: Did the cat simply wander off at the picnic stop, then panic and vanish into the undergrowth nearby? Did the cat deliberately rebel and set off for home? And how, for goodness sake, did the cat find its way from Santa Barbara, California, to its old home street in Portland, Oregon? With cars, trucks, and buses, not to mention hawks, owls, eagles, dogs, and wildlife like foxes and coyotes, how did the animal survive the journey and how did it navigate? One might also ask *why?*

There are even stranger *"incredible journeys"* reported where people move away, perhaps from Chicago to New Orleans, and leave their cat with relatives or friends, only to have the cat abandon its new home and show up on the doorstep of its original family's new home a thousand or more miles away. Coast-to-coast trips have abounded in story after story, all dressed as non-fiction.

Collectively, these wondrous happenings are called psi-trailing by some observers, and have to be accepted on trust if they are to be accepted at all. They are anecdotes, and anecdotes do not a science make. On the other hand, to reject them is to state a negative, "The cat did not make the trip from its new home in Chicago to its original family's new home near New Orleans," and negatives are never provable. Scientifically, negatives have to be converted to a positive or are not acceptable as evidence. Can we say, "That cat stayed right where it belonged in its new home in Chicago until it died of old age years later"? Or, perhaps, "The original owners of the cat never had a cat live with them again once they moved to Louisiana"? Either of those statements could be provable, but not a statement that said the cat never made the trip.

What we have, then, is our own willingness to accept on trust what people tell us in these wonderful anecdotes, and they are full of wonder if they are true even a fraction of the time. Ironically, if any one of these psi-trailing stories is true—particularly where an animal finds its family (as in the trip from Chicago to New Orleans) without prior experience, as opposed to retracing steps taken (albeit in a car or other non-biological conveyance) as in the trip back to Portland from Santa Barbara—if even one is true, then all the stories we have heard over the millennia have the potential of truth in them. If there is a way for any cat to do such things, then all cats, presumably, have the same equipment, whatever that might be. Acceptance or rejection should be a slow and deliberate process. As for the cats that simply vanish and never turn up, that could be because of

the mortality rate on the road. We listed hazards both natural and unnatural for the cat that vanished near Santa Barbara. We must assume that the hazards win most of the time and no one is ever the wiser. We don't know what happened to the cat, sad to say, and the cat died learning its lesson.

Perhaps the easiest part to understand is motivation. That is readily explained. Cats don't like change without their consent. Cats are forever rejecting out of hand things we do like trying them on a new food, packing our suitcases, and heaven only knows they can be sulky and out of sorts when we do nothing more malicious than move a few pieces of furniture around. Changing homes altogether may be more than some cats are willing to accept. We are not at all certain how they perceive such changes, what messages they send up to their central control for evaluation and instructions. That is one reason knowledgeable cat people suggest keeping an indoor-outdoor cat inside a new home for a week or more at least before letting it explore around outside in new surroundings. We'll come to the reason for that shortly. (Cats should only be allowed outdoors, in my opinion, when there is land to accommodate them that will keep them away from the road. Cats are generally idiots when it comes to traffic. They just don't believe in it so therefore it is not there. They are no better than skunks in that regard.)

Any cat, then, might try to correct an obvious wrong and head for the home it knows and loves and, more importantly, trusts. Navigation should not be too much of a problem. A cat probably has a built-in direction finder based on the sun. If you move a cat two hundred miles away from its familiar zone, you can throw the angle of the sun off by a significant degree. A cat sensitive to that change would almost certainly move in the one direction that tended to correct the change, i.e., towards familiar home ground. That sun compass may be what puts homing pigeons on the tack for home, and why should we accept that ability in a bird brain and not in a cat? As we shall see, there may be other navigational factors, but a natural tendency to correct discrepancies in sun angle could be a big part of it. There is nothing spooky or arcane about that. It is just one more unknown factor in what is almost certainly a grand array of devices and systems.

When we say sun, we usually take that to mean the sun giving off the light we perceive and understand. That is a very limited part of the spectrum. Again, seeking an animal analogue, there is a small island off the east coast of New Zealand called Campbell and on it is the last known population of a now rare form of reptiles known as tuatara. They look like lizards but are not truly so. They belong to a reptilian group that was once widespread all around our planet perhaps 150 to 200 million years ago. They began their journey to extinction about the time the dinosaurs did, but unlike the dinosaurs left this provable vestige population. (There are claims that a vestige population of dinosaurs remains in the Congo but we have nothing like proof of that. We do have the tuatara, however. I have held one and it was still squirming with vigour and ill-temper. Neither their disposition nor their texture has improved with age.)

One of the things that distinguishes the tuatara (and the modern lizards, too, for that matter) is a kind of third eye. It is called the pineal eye. It is between and somewhat above the line of the normal reptilian eye pair. We are certain that the tuatara doesn't see images with this tiny vestige, but it is believed it is able to detect infrared light or at least light from one extreme end of the spectrum that is well beyond the human detection zone. Just what the tuatara does with infrared light is not known, but it does indicate that at least some animals have the ability to deal with environmental data that we do not believe we have. Perhaps cats detect way-out ends of the spectrum and use that information for navigation or some other purpose. It is certainly not something we understand well enough to define or accept or reject. We do know some animals deal with some data we can't absorb in any conscious way. There are other worlds that we can only guess at and those are the worlds where cats live and from whose heights they look down on us. If all that seems to be a bit Olympian we must remember that at the time Olympus was established as god-country, cats, too, were objects of adoration if not actual worship. That may not be coincidence. The history of the domestic cat is not long, little more than four thousand years, but much of it has been secret and not just a little of it locked away in rituals of the human mind.

Many years ago, while working on a book, I visited the scientific research station at the geographical South Pole. I was shown a series of maps of the Antarctic continent covered with lines of apparently random shape. They enclosed areas of widely varying size. The lines looked like the outlines of partially collapsed balloons. More specifically, they looked like topographical maps I had seen giving altitudes in a very bumpy mountain range. It was not altitude that was shown on those maps, however, but magnetic fields, and what was displayed there is true of the entire surface of our planet. Foot by foot, mile by mile, and perhaps inch by inch, the magnetic intensity of our planet varies no matter which way one moves. I have long believed that animals migrate at least in part by being aware of the magnetism of our planet and moving toward fields they know by experience or instinct are where they ought to be. California grey whales migrate over ten thousand miles a year, the Arctic tern migrates at least twice that distance, salmon head out to sea for as long as seven years and then head home to the very gravel beds where they were spawned. With pollution at its present revolting high, animals are unlikely to be able to taste or smell their way. There has to be one or more other guiding systems, and I have long felt magnetism was at least one of them. As with the number of senses animals have, once we leave that safe, known number of five behind we have opened a gate and almost anything could come tumbling through from the vast storehouse of phenomena we know as the unknown. Quite simply we don't have the foggiest notion how many ways animals have to navigate seasonally, singly, or in combinations we can only wonder about. We don't know enough about it all even to guess very intelligently. That could work for cats as well as for whales or terns, salmon or hummingbirds or Monarch butterflies.

We can use the dog as a reasonable analogue. We maintain two residences and when the kids were still at school we utilised both. Every Friday we loaded dogs and cats and a weekend's worth of groceries into the estate car and headed out to the beach house. The animals settled down and slept. When we got to within two or three miles of the house, the dogs were up crying and squirming with excitement. Could they have known where we were by elapsed time? No. Categorically, no. Sometimes we stopped on the way to see friends, sometimes we stopped to shop or eat, and traffic conditions varied greatly. Time simply could not have been a factor. Could the dogs have seen something out of the windows of the car? No, it was virtually always dark when we arrived, and besides a dog just doesn't have the kind of eyes that would function on rapidly moving objects at a distance of fifty or more feet. To complicate matters, we didn't always go by the same route. We had several options depending on traffic or plans to stop off along the way. No, not sight signals.

Sound, perhaps? That can't be as readily ruled out. Tyres make different noises on different stretches of road surface but that doesn't seem likely, somehow. Nothing outside the car as we moved along country roads except the possibility of tyre noise should have been able to alert them. And as for smell, most unlikely. The carbon fumes from the car almost certainly would have masked anything outside the car.

Magnetism seemed then and still seems now to be the most likely signals for the dogs to have read. The same could be true for cats. In the car trips I have described, the cats were in carrying cases for safety reasons when we stopped along the way and opened the car doors. Looking back, I am not certain how they reacted to being near our house. The dogs were typically bumptious and noisy over how they felt about things. It is the belief that cats do imprint on local magnetism that prompts the suggestion that they be kept in for several days or even a week in a new home. Then, when they do go out, they will know they have a home base when it comes time to backtrack. They will have absorbed the location of that all-important square one and have memorised its magnetic "shape".

And there is yet another very arcane way that cats could possibly maintain a far more intimate relationship with the real world than we do, although we know so very little about it all that we can only guess. This is rather in line with my conversation with Professor Good on the subject of precognition. We have to go back down to subatomic particles.

A tiny mote of dust is truly a cosmos unto itself, that much we do now know. It contains molecules that are far too small for us to see without a microscope, but they are no less real than the dust itself or the piano on which the mote of dust has settled. Each of those molecules which is yet another universe within ever-diminishing universes has a nucleus at least as much smaller than the molecule as the molecule is than the dust speck and the dust speck the house in which it is found. Far, far smaller than the nucleus are atoms racing around that core at insane speeds, at more millions of miles an hour than we might care to contemplate. There are some we can't really see without elaborate equipment that can take us to absolutely huge orders of magnification. We can track those atoms because of the energy they emit, they being energy themselves.

Well beyond the atoms in the diminishing order of matter and energy there are subatomic particles, and they are so small we have to detect them by complex electronic means or simply by prediction. We really do anticipate them more than we see them. Then there are sub-subatomic particles, and we are not at all sure where if anywhere it all might end. In all likelihood it never ends and we have come thereby to the threshold of eternity. What is important is that at some point, matter ceases to be matter in the way the piano and the dust mote are and it all becomes energy screaming around on some predetermined track through time and space.

Some people suggest that at that stage energy is really a set of harmonics and that, in a sense, that is really a kind of celestial music that comes up up up through the scale of things until it becomes matter— eventually the dust mote and the piano and the house and the city and the planet and the solar system and the universe and the cosmos. It works the same way in either direction, up or down. But where it all starts, far, far down the scale in size, it is a tone, not a solid hunk of something. If matter, then, at some point is sound, is there any way the cat or any other animal

could tune in on it? On the surface of it, it doesn't seem remotely possible. In the reality of it, we haven't even a remote idea. Cats are connected to both reality and unreality in some way or ways we don't understand at all. Any avenue, then, is worth exploring, even if it takes us down down down into the hollowness between solar systems which is apparently a direct analogue of the hollowness between the particles that make up the world we can reach out and touch.

If this seems a little on the spooky side because of its minuteness, then so is astronomy for precisely the opposite reason. Imagine light travelling at 196 million miles a second, taking 100 billion years to get here and tell us what was happening that long before our planet was formed. The moment you move up or down from where we are and what we can see and touch, you are getting spooky. We are all suspended precariously in between that ultimate big and the ultimate small, all of us including cats. Who can say where other species plug in and whence they take their clues? The only spooky thing about all this is the belief some people hold that they can make definite statements about what is and what is not, what can be and what cannot be. There has to be a point when we get even a little bit modest and where "I don't know" is the most intelligent of all utterances.

To put this in perspective: They tell the story of that proverbial little old lady in sensible walking shoes who attended a lecture given by a venerable and extremely wise college professor on the origin of the universe. He spoke of the *big bang* and quasars and pulsars and black holes and all of the other recent darlings of physicists. When it was all over and the people were filing out of the hall with puzzled looks on their faces, our little old lady approached the professor and advised him he had it all wrong. "Oh?" he said, obviously amused. "Yes," said the lady, "the world is sitting on the back of a turtle." "And what is the turtle standing on?" the increasingly amused scientist asked. "Another turtle," was the reply. "And that turtle?" "Look, sonny, save your breath. It's turtles all the way down." Perhaps for cats it is just that, turtles all the way down. It could help explain a lot about cats, about turtles, and about our cosmos. I am not at all certain what it might say about us.

There can be a tendency toward embarrassment as we enter these more arcane considerations of how cats might read the world around them. Are we standing on a distant windblown hilltop holding Shirley Maclaine's hand waiting for the songs of the stars to come to us? Or are we poking a little ahead of conventional wisdom as presently defined? I think the latter. A hundred years ago talk of subnuclear particles could have got one referred, if not instantly confined. Five hundred years ago it could have got one burned at the stake or subjected to some other equally unsuitable form of religious soul cleansing. How would you like to have tried to explain atom smashing to Sir Thomas More or his friend Erasmus? But all that has become "conventional wisdom" and there do not seem to be any restrictions against going on further. I read recently that one of our contemporary resident geniuses on earth, Edward Fredkin, says the whole cosmos is a computer and we are but figments of some chip's imagination, or fragments. In 1960 the Astronomer Royal of England (poor dear, imagine living with this one for the rest of your life!) said that all the current blather about astronautics was "pure poppy-cock". No, there doesn't appear to be the old dread that there once was of falling off the edge of the earth if you sail too far. The very concept of "too far". It is all out there to be discovered, and to discover the link of the cat should that time ever arrive, it will be shown that there never was a "too far." It is all out there to be discovered, and to discover the link of the cat to its reality we are going to have to sail a lot further than we have gone so far. We are going to have to dare to dare, or we shall never find our total cat. But then, if you are a cat owner, unabashed and unafraid, you know that already. Just hug your cat and apologise for what you are about to do—pry.

As this portion of the book is being written a new kitten has entered our circle, an eight-week-old male blue-point Siamese we have named Sumay. (The meaning of that name is a profoundly secret, extremely deep and personal family affair. It is known to us and the National Security Agency only. I dare not speak of it here.)

Sumay has all of his conventional senses on line. His eyes have been open for perhaps six and a half weeks, his ears for approximately as long, and his nose and sense of touch for his full eight weeks. We don't know exactly when his ability to really taste things become operative, but since it is so closely linked to the early-active sense of smell and is so involved with eating, we believe it easily predates both hearing and sight. At any rate, in a very small package with ears far too big to match his head or body, Sumay has come to rest with a family who will guard him for life. It has given us the opportunity to watch him explore not only this house but this world. It is all new and he has set about absorbing as much as possible in the shortest time possible.

The first objects for discovery and exploration for Sumay were animals with just two legs. We tower over him, speak at a decibel count that must be totally astounding to him, and we pick him up, handle him, pass him around, and at the relatively few ounces he weighs there isn't a lot he can do about it. His first problem was to determine whether all of this is good for Siamese kittens or bad. Surely he has encountered people before, but now his mother and littermates are missing from the scene and this little mite has to face the world square on, on his own. He decided within an hour or so that people are good for kittens and that being passive really isn't the way the game was meant to be played. Within the first two hours he was jumping up onto couches and seeking out a lap to curl up on. And he was purring as soon as he was cuddling. People scooping him up were invitations to snuggle in close, and a straight charge across the floor with tail pointed straight up—a very skinny tail it is, too—is the way to get scooped up. He cuddles and he purrs in total contentment at every possible opportunity and has become, in just two days, a terrible time waster. We have repeatedly found our housekeeper sitting in a far corner of the sunroom playing with this small feline. Fingers dragged across a cushion are already perceived as an invitation to a game.

Consider what has happened here. I would guess the kitten weighs about a pound, I weigh over two hundred. Flat on his four feet he towers perhaps six or seven inches into the air and I tower roughly twelve times that height. His voice is a small *mewwww* or purr, and my voice is loud, thunderous when compared to his, and what I say, the sounds I make, must be unintelligible to him. Some day some of it will make sense, but not in two days. Yet this kitten with cognitive powers considered to be far below our own has worked out what is good and what is bad.

An example of the bad? Last night he was carefully exploring a windowsill eight feet long. Suddenly there appeared from the dark beyond, suspended in air, a kitten just exactly like himself. It was on the other side of the glass mimicking Sumay's every move. That startled Sumay and that in turn made him angry. He hesitated for only a moment and then made a terrible face as he spat. It wasn't all that impressive a spit as spits go, but then Sumay is very tiny. It sounded rather like *pitsitz*. The other cat, with its head at exactly the same angle but as a mirror image, spat back, and although the spit beyond the glass could not be heard, the expression was exactly the same as Sumay's. Sumay and the strange, threatening foe levitating beyond that glass were nose to nose. The angry face on the other side of the strange barrier shook Sumay up so badly that it made him fall off the windowsill all the way to the living room floor and that made the little Siamese terror even angrier. And all of this made him need cuddling even more than usual, but he still spits and hums very angry sounds when he is carried past the window where that other kitten, his identical twin, caused him such anxiety and indignity. So Sumay, at eight weeks, knows there is good and there is bad, and he will be on the lookout for both as long as he lives. It is very important that cats learn as soon as possible that both forces are at work, and it is absolutely essential that they be able to distinguish between the two and react appropriately. This information is stored in some way. Sumay's brain will have to be able to distinguish between the forces of dark and light but will not have to work them out every time either is encountered. The cat does not remember and make associations as we do, so far as we know, but some associations, certain basic survival data, are stored. It is very difficult to determine from the outside looking in what data is from experiences achieved and what has worked its way into genetic data over the millennia.

It seems to me that if you or I were picked up by strangers, put in a box, put aboard a space ship (isn't a motor car to a kitten what a flying saucer would be to us—beyond any previous experience and therefore entirely beyond comprehension?) and then unloaded into a building, where absolutely nothing is familiar we would at least "freak out". This strange new place after all is occupied by enormous giants—creatures twelve times our height and two hundred times our bulk—things with thunderingly loud voices uttering sounds with no relationship to the sounds we heard from our mothers and littermates—could we sort it out in forty-eight hours using just our five senses? I think we could not do what Sumay has done and I don't for a moment think Sumay has done it with just five senses either. Somehow he has been able to tune in in a way we don't understand and work things out that assure him not only of survival but of comfort. He knows what his little dish means when it is brought down off the worktop and put on the floor. That is instinct, in all probability, because he started eating shortly after being born. But he already knows which worktop the dish will come down from, and that isn't instinct. His mother didn't use dishes. He uses a litter tray, runs to it when in need, and he knows how to drink liquids that come from a cold dish rather than a warm fountain. Fortunately, all of that is child's play to an eight-week-old kitten because that kitten is a child of his own kind. He has been programmed by his species history to handle all of these things

very quickly or get out of the way. Other kittens are waiting to take a failure's place.

Now there are other animals. He spits at some of the grown cats, which is fine because that means that all-important self-socialisation has begun, and the sooner that happens the better. The grown cats are typically afraid of him and back off. Nature may have built that apparent bit of silliness into cats for a good reason. An immediate attitude of being intimidated on the part of older cats (apparently baseless given the animals' respective sizes) allows the kitten a few days of grace. By the time the kitten has the hang of living in close quarters with other animals, the larger specimens will have come to tolerate the newcomer and will have either started parenting it or ignoring it. Either way the frightened little creature can act with all the bravado it feels it must display without triggering a serious confrontation or even death. In politics it is what is known as a honeymoon.

Last night Lizzie our basset hound was allowed into the same room with Sumay and after an initial "*what the hell is that?*" Sumay settled right down. Using whatever deep probes he has in his receiver array, he came up with a positive reading. The sixty-pound basset is as okay as we are. The smell of it may not be exactly perfect to a kitten but it is warm, not at all aggressive and obviously comes as part of the package. The other cats and dogs will be introduced one at a time, leaving the most bumptious for last. They have all seen too many other animals on their turf for too many years to be threatening to the kitten except through good spirits. The great big dogs like the 120-pound bloodhounds know about their size and power somehow and will be careful. They always are with small animals. Most giants are. The smaller terriers like the petite basset griffon vendeen are less likely to exhibit reserve. Their *joi* over a new playmate will be boundless, but then, they are French.

Through all of this there has been this handful of kitten receiving enormous numbers of signals, sorting them out, reacting to them, and swaggering up to each monster-size challenge confident, apparently, that it knows all it has to know or at least can learn all it has to learn instantaneously. Since taste and touch have not played a major role in the evaluations that have been guiding Sumay, can we really believe that three known ports of input—sight, sound, and smell—have been enough for the kitten to tune in through? We speak of ourselves getting good and bad *vibes* when we meet new people. I am not sure if that implies extrasensory ports because we do hear languages we understand, we can read voice tone and body language, we know warm and welcoming from snide and denigrating. We know innuendo, we comprehend sarcasm, we can determine political content, and very often we have some historical basis for the individual we are meeting. It probably matters that we can't stand his parents or used to date her mother. People come with baggage. Also, people look like people we have known before and that certainly is a factor in how we accept or reject people newly met. Jill went to grammar school with a boy named Alec and this poor little tyke wet his pants virtually every day. To this day my wife with her typical long memory has trouble relating to men named Alec. She always expects the worst and gets the giggles.

But Sumay is fifty-eight days old. His eyesight can hardly encompass our full sizes in one big visual bite. Clearly, he must see us piecemeal, he hears nothing intelligible, we don't know how to hum and purr very effectively, and we are, again, much, much too loud for normal interkitten communication. How does Sumay get his vibes? It is certain that he does. He has already started to pick out preferred people, he instantly picked out cats from other cats and put the basset down as perfectly okay. He has limited powers of cognition because he doesn't have the large, recently evolved lobes that we have. He can't talk it over with himself, as far as we know, and there is no substitute that we can envisage for introspection and consciously weighing pros and cons, creating good and bad columns. At something like gut level this two-month-old kitten is able to take in data by means not known to us and get an almost immediate turnround. In a less benign environment, that turnround time and the accuracy of what came back from central control in the form of instructions would be likely to mean the difference between life and death.

Sumay isn't going to get mauled for a bad reading but he is making readings anyway, somehow, at near the speed of light. Our catalogue of senses, even our catalogue of possible senses, just can't explain it. You don't get vibes by banging on empty air. Sumay, even at his very tender age, has been doing much more than that. He has been calling on resources we don't know about and absorbing data we obviously can't detect. He is pulling things out of the sensory maze and isolating them, using them. It is a little like looking at a paisley fabric. No one of us can ever know what any other person is actually seeing, even when we are all seeing it at the same time from the same angle in the same light. We may all say that it is pretty, but what is pretty and why is a private set of stimulations and reactions, interpretations, if you will. In some kind of a final analysis, each of us lives alone in an isolated sensory world. The only people who even try to communicate what they have encountered behind their eyes are those strange but wonderful people we call poets. That is one good reason why we should cherish them so.

Drawing by Steinlen

10

We have owned Thistle Hill Farm for just a little over a month as this is being written. When we took over, we found two horses in terrible condition and a collie held in such little regard by the farm's former owners that although it had lived here for nine years, it had never been given a name. It had also never been in the house and was virtually never fed. It had to forage on its own and beg on nearby farms. Our daughter took the collie to her farm and spent over three hundred dollars in veterinary bills getting her spayed, dewormed, and given the first protective shots she had ever had. It is a wonder she had lived under those conditions for nearly a decade. This is horse country and wandering dogs very often get shot. Few breeders are tolerant of dogs that seek recreation by chasing half-million-dollar studs through fences or into farm machinery. The poor wretch also had most of the skin ailments known to affect dogdom and a few the vet hadn't heard of. The neighbours say she has had litter after litter of puppies over the years, encounters with wandering dogs no doubt, but no one ever saw the puppies. It is assumed that they were killed. The collie is now called Fontine and is the ultimate sofa-hogger at our daughter's place. At least from nine on, she can have a thoroughly luxurious life. She actually shows how very grateful she is at every opportunity.

As one might expect under such conditions, there is a cadre of feral cats here as well. They are not as amenable to contact as Fontine was. So far no one has been able to touch one. They will soon be trapped (in a box trap), spayed or neutered, and then released back to the barn after being dewormed and given all the shots they need. It is unlikely but not wholly out of the question that they would ever settle down and accept human beings as reliable companions. We are told that an uncountable number of cats were born here over the years, but they were never spayed or altered, never given shots or otherwise handled, and never fed. They lived on mice, rats, voles and moles, and one suspects chipmunks, squirrels, and songbirds. We have already found two dead and quite thoroughly petrified cats, one in a woodpile and one with its head stuck in a clothes-dryer vent. The poor creature had apparently gone there to get warm some winter long ago.

What we have, then, is a flock of cats that have no reason at all to trust us or to like us even a little bit. All humans who come from this house must be bad news to them, or at least are not harbingers of good news like food and concern.* The people they had known before us, at least from this house, certainly offered them little enough in kindness or favours. We have counted four cats so far, one all black and three quite lovely-looking cats apparently of one strain. They are white, very white, with patches of mixed red and black brindle. We assume one of the three is the mother and the others two of her surviving kittens. Heaven only knows what happened to all of the others over the years.

Our feral cats are fed now on a regular basis, and although they will suddenly appear at the head of a tunnel in a mountain of straw bales to watch us fill their dish, they won't let us even start to get near them. No way, no touching. All any of us has to do is turn and face them and they are gone. The speed with which they can retreat into their secret passageways is almost magic. One moment they are there and the next there is not even a track to prove that they ever lived. They are of the stuff of which apparitions are made. About an hour ago I looked up from my computer at a hillside outside my study window and one of the white-plus cats was sitting staring in at me. It was there for a moment and then, *poof*, it was gone. It was looking directly at me, though, it was watching, and we made eye contact. It could be a beginning, I suppose, but those cats will have to make the first moves. If I do, I am certain to spook them. They have a lot of watching to do before they decide on a first tentative approach, should they decide on making contact at all.

These cats are not playing games as far as I can tell. They are watching and judging the changes that have been made, and to them it is apparently a critical task. There are good signs. All of a sudden there is a regular food

---

* A kind neighbour did sneak over and leave food for them when the house here was empty.

dish, something they had not always been able to rely on before. Every day it is filled. There is a water dish. It is no longer necessary to work down through the brambles to get to the stream. Not one of the new crew has thrown anything at them and we have not been overly insistent that we make physical contact, something we are certain would upset them. We seem to be accepting life together in *our* barn on their terms. That's all right, though, there is room enough for all and time enough for all parties to work things out.

The operative word here, though, is watching. If we go out in the evening they are sitting near the barn. When we open the car door on our return, they vanish, but they were there waiting for us to come back. If we let the dogs out, the cats are watching. Today I took a long walk down near the marsh and back through the woods. Twice I spotted a cat sitting on a hillside in an overlooking pasture, just looking. Late this afternoon, a neighbour with a paving business called to give us an estimate on what it would cost to tarmac our driveway and the aisle between the stalls. At least twice I saw cats watching us. On one occasion our border collie forgot his training and chased one of the white-plus jobs up a tree. While the dog got roundly scolded, the cat settled in on a low branch and continued checking us out from there. A dog chasing them is obviously a matter of little account. These are cats that know how to survive. I have the feeling that if Duncan had somehow caught up with the cat, we would have had to take Duncan in for stitches.

I am sure the Thistle Hill Regulars come near the house at night and try to pick up audio clues as to what we are all about. In fact they appear to be just about everywhere we go, and that isn't easy. We have two and a half miles of fences and four buildings, woods, streams, meadows, pastures, a lot of complex topography, and yet one or more of the four cats is always there no matter where we walk, which way we turn. Our cats are doing more than just watching us; they are trying to figure us out. Perhaps they work in shifts or in assigned geographical regions. I wonder how they pool the data they collect.

Since the cats we brought with us to Thistle Hill are sleek and happy, we are, in fact, worth finding out about. It is possible that the outside cats may already know about the feline newcomers, but how that could be I just don't know, unless their sense of smell alone has tipped them off. Still the scrutiny continues. It is quiet, unobtrusive, and certainly not

threatening, simply persistent. Although it all happens in a silent and almost slow-motion way, it carries a sense of urgency. I have never heard any of the Regulars utter a sound. Silence makes watching even more intense, somehow.

If someone or something is trying to find out about you, then it stands to reason that you might be curious about the attention you are getting and its source. Why are the old Thistle Hill Farm cats so intent on knowing all there is to learn about us? Check through those things that we know motivate interest. *Sex.* Certainly not that, although all of the Regulars here will be trapped and spayed or neutered before being turned back loose on the local barn rats and mice. Still, whatever the state their reproductive organs may be in, the cats of Thistle Hill have no sexual interest in us. *Food.* Are we prey or potential prey? That is as far-fetched a hypothesis as the suggestion that sex could be the attraction. The former owners, as mentioned, did not bother to feed the cats as we do every day without fail. But that kindly neighbour, Ditty Gentry by name, who loves all animals, not just her own, did feed them often, so it is not as if food made a sudden appearance. Food has appeared from time to time and I don't think the cats are curious about that. There are streams here at Thistle Hill, so water has not been an issue. With many forms of wildlife, especially during drought conditions, water can be the most important single issue of all, but that has nothing to do with matters here. And the cats of Thistle Hill have the same shelter they have always had, so that isn't anything they have to wonder about. We are not noisy and certainly no more threatening to the cats than the cats are to us. Our only interaction is that we do talk to them when we see them, at least we make what we hope are reassuring *kitty-kitty* sounds when we see them. It seems neighbourly. They don't respond except by fleeing, yet a few minutes later they will be back watching us again. It goes on late into the night and often, when I go to turn off the outside light at the far end of the front walk, I take one last look out of the window before hitting the switch and at least one of the cats will be sitting there looking at the house. Again, I pose the question, *why*?

If some day the Thistle Hill Regulars allow us to make contact with them, I suppose the question will answer itself. They are simply building up nerve and deciding either to make the move or to allow us to make one. It can't be the fact that we have cats inside, even if they can smell them, because all of this started before any of our cats were moved down here from Long Island.

Day and night, then, three or four cats are watching us, and when they can't see any of us they are watching the buildings that have apparently swallowed us up. If someone feared cats, I suppose all this intense scrutiny would be upsetting. It would have some of the quality of *Bell, Book and Candle*. Since we have never got into witches and their familiars, for this family of animal lovers it is a wonderful game. We are sure, with the only problem being we don't understand the rules or the goals, that it is somehow structured. Is the next move ours, and if so what should it be? We will shortly be making a shocking move when we trap them, have them neutered and otherwise medicated. But that trauma will be short-lived and only the earliest phase will apparently involve us. The rest, the heavy-duty parts, will be handled by strangers at a veterinary hospital who will be as intent as we will be on not being flayed alive. The cats of Thistle Hill are all quite handsome, but I am sure would be demons if grabbed with bare hands.

The only conclusion I can come to is that the Thistle Hill Regulars find us amusing or at least in some vague way entertaining. If they do have the power of anticipation, perhaps they expect us to do something weird. The answer could lie in a past we don't understand. It is possible that previous owners did unpleasant things like throw stones at them (we do not actually know that to be the case) and the Regulars are waiting to see what nasty tricks we know. That is supposition, however.

We have here at Thistle Hill a perfect example of cats awatching, four of them, for reasons they alone understand, if indeed they understand it themselves. We suspect they do, somehow. Cats are curious, of course, but the Regulars have had weeks to satisfy their curiosities. We must be a bit of a disappointment to them because so far we haven't done anything peculiar at all. Because we know how their standard array of senses works, we can pretty well figure out what they see and hear, smell and would be able to taste and touch. We don't know what part magnetism or the far ends of the light spectrum might be revealing to them, and as for the harmonics of the sub-sub-subminiature parts of the universe that not only surround us but constitute our physical matter, who knows? That is as far removed from the reality of our relationship as our understanding of the Regulars' motives.

One of the white-plus cats has just come into view again on the hill outside my study window. He has seated himself in the same place he was yesterday and he is looking directly into my window. In fact, I think we are making eye contact for the second day in a row. I don't know why but somehow I think he does. I think I will see how long it takes to stare him down. (In a way I lost. A phone call came in from my agent and I had to take some notes. When I looked up, my spy friend was walking away.)

Lilly is an example of how this checking-into business can pay off. Before my daughter and her husband got their place up here in horse country, they owned a home on a quiet street in suburban Baltimore. As always they had cats and dogs, and they had an invaluable adjunct, a fenced garden. Periodically a pretty but fairly nondescript medium-coated cat appeared on their front porch or in the back garden.

Eventually she began coming into the house with the acknowledged resident cats. She didn't stay long, usually, but she would eat and drink and even napped a few times. She could be petted, even picked up, and was only slightly aloof. She seemed to be looking things over or thinking them through.

Thinking she might belong to someone further down the street and be missed, my daughter began asking house-to-house as time allowed. No one claimed ownership but any number of families had or were having the same experience with the wanderer. She slept first in one house and then another, ate where she felt like eating, and was so pleasant that no one seemed to mind. Eventually she began sleeping at my daughter and her husband's place and was given the interim name of Lilly. For weeks she came and went. She could be gone for days, sometimes for no more than hours. It got to the point where Pamela and Joe began worrying if she didn't show up. Then one day she checked in bag and baggage and that was that. She began using the inside litter tray as her regular comfort station and showed no inclination to visit old friends up and down the block. She had insinuated herself as gracefully as one could wish. She never left the house and garden again, and when it came time to move, Lilly went along. The new place is apparently fine with her, too.

Clearly, or at least it seems clear to me, Lilly was checking out what the neighbourhood had to offer. No one knows where she came from but she wandered in, or was dropped off and abandoned, who knows? The point

is, she had to make new living arrangements before winter. I shouldn't think she understood that imperative, but she made her choice, a choice that meant survival if it were a good one. On what did she base her solution to life's latest little problem? Was it the menu, the temperature at which the house was maintained, the human family, the animal family? According to Pamela, the other homes she had been using off and on seemed to offer as much in the way of creature comforts as their home. Still, Lilly kept her own clipboard, made her own notes and evaluations, and chose. She chose well, but we can never know what scale of points she used. Just like the Thistle Hill Regulars, she watched, and because she had been socialised at some point in her life, she even touched. She is, by the way, a delightful cat. And no one can accuse her of not knowing how to put her world together. When you see her curled up by the fire or on the foot of my granddaughter's bed or rubbing up against Fontine the collie or Zack the Labrador retriever purring, you have to grant her her survival skills.

I know of a more surprising case three thousand miles away in a very different world, Brentwood, just west of Beverly Hills. There has occurred there a stunning victory for catkind and it is very revealing for anyone interested in the ways of these creatures.

Charlie and Jane Powell (he claims to have married her so he could tell everyone he was married to *Jane Powell*, which dates him) were children of Manhattan. They were both raised in the heart of New York City, in apartments, the children of two non-animal-orientated families although they were culturally enriched in all other ways. There is nothing wrong with that (I suppose) but it does create a kind of person who will very often stay in and repeat that mould.

Then came Mel (now an attorney and that dates all of us) and it became evident that he would have to be an only child. Jane and Charlie, he a motion-picture executive and she a book editor, were well read enough to know how much a pet was supposed to mean to a child, especially an only child, and although it was not a concept they knew by instinct or from first-hand experience, they decided to do what they were sure was right. Mel was to be denied nothing and such in fact has been the case. With absolutely no more personal enthusiasm for the job than they would have experienced contracting a nappy service (which dates me), they bought a puppy, an easy keeper for an apartment, a vest pocket-sized Yorkshire terrier, Little Nell. Before they quite realised what had happened they were in love, deeply so. They did not feign amazement, they were amazed! As it turned out, they had both been closet animal lovers all along without either of them having the remotest clue that they were carrying the bug. It was a joy to behold. Those of us who had grown up with animals just nodded knowingly and watched the pleasant scene unfold.

In good time the inevitable call from Hollywood came and the Powells with Mel and Nell in tow headed west. After Little Nell met an unexpected and unhappy fate in a freak accident, there was another Yorkie who managed to live out a good, full life. Before a third dog could be selected, something happened that changed everything. It was as unanticipated as their adoration of Little Nell. Somewhere high in the clouds a finger or perhaps a paw was pointed downward towards a beautiful house in Brentwood and the Powells were chosen. One has to believe the match was made in Heaven, or was at least foreordained.

Their very nice home with its swimming pool and manicured gardens was being cased by a dark and handsome but secretive stranger. Day and night, we must surmise, he who was to become known as Seymour moved through their shrubbery and among their flower beds. Seymour-to-be was a black tom cat whose origins and early experiences are the secrets of the gods of the cats and not knowable. Eventually Seymour let himself be seen and then he began to hang around in the open near the patio. Well, the Powells, reckoned, the swimming-pool water, full of chemicals as it always is, can't be good for a cat, so a bowl, a cut-glass bowl, a once upon a time wedding present as I recall, was put out with the water changed several times a day. A small enough comfort to offer a stranger perhaps from out of town.

Then one day Jane was shopping and passed the pet food aisle in the supermarket. Why not? She bought the most expensive brand of cat food they had to offer and some toys. Again, why not? So Seymour, now duly dubbed thus, was eating and drinking just outside the sliding patio doors. What happened next was inevitable. Someone en route to or from the pool left a slider slightly ajar and Seymour the moocher stepped inside never to leave again. He found a nicely puffed-up chair with a pleasing view and settled in. Then came the cat tray, the litter, more toys, and a visit to the vet. *Voilà!* The Powells with renewed amazement realised they adored cats, too. They hadn't had even a clue, not a tic or a murmur before Seymour joined the family.

We have to see Seymour in context. A check around indicated that a large jet black cat had been seen in the neighbourhood in the preceding two weeks or so but he had no known home. For a cat to survive in that particular area is close to miraculous. In the surrounding hills and valleys there is a great deal of urban wildlife, including plenty of coyotes who love a good haunch of domestic cat for lunch. (They also like small dogs, so keeping the likes of toy poodles and cats can be tricky when supervision is casual.) In the hills, although their kind has been so badly persecuted their days in the area are numbered, there are rattlesnakes who don't hunt cats, certainly, but deeply resent cats who hunt them. Cats do hunt snakes for fun if not for food and are not very good at distinguishing venomous from non-venomous species. There are feral dogs, of course, but even worse for cats are the many estates that have guard dogs on patrol off lead. The Powells' home is only about four long city blocks north of Sunset Boulevard, and that wagon track is suicidal to cross in anything less than a tank, and so, for that matter, are the avenues and streets that cross and feed into it. For Seymour to have spent any time at all as a wanderer in the Brentwood/Westwood area and to have achieved his adulthood, if that is where he grew up on his own, was amazing. But he may have done just that.

Before Charlie and Jane could totally understand what had happened to them, Katt appeared just as Seymour had. Katt is another jet black male cat and a very handsome beast, too. The only way he can be distinguished from Seymour is by his golden eyes. Seymour's are distinctly green. Heaven only knows where Katt came from or how he survived either, but there he is in the house living as high as Seymour is, both of them in peace and harmony. Some months later another cat I never met appeared but quickly succumbed to what the vet assured Charlie and Jane was a wholly intractable urinary disorder.

Then, suddenly, Arby appeared. She is a marmalade job, about the same size as the boys and just as pleasant. They are all remarkable moochers. Before the Powells had quite understood that they owned three cats where neither of them had ever dreamed that they would own one, they somehow got shanghaied into a shelter and adopted their first kitten, a remarkable tortoiseshell named Moca.

But, back to the first four, the three that lived and the one that didn't.

Had word got around? Could there be an underground signal system that puts the news out, *"Good pickings over on Homewood Way"*? Or is it possible that cats really are watching that carefully and know or find out for themselves where the easy touches are to be found? If there are a number of cats in one home, other cats might hone in on the smell or even pick up clues from kitty litter put out with the rubbish. But how does it start from ground zero? I think one cat gives the place a try and the other cats that wander by are on the lookout. Cats really are watching. That is the least spooky way to account for a case like Pamela, Joe, Sarah, and Lilly, and another like the Powells.

Several remarkable things have apparently occurred there in Brentwood. The cats, one at a time, for they came singly and well spaced, picked the Powell household although initially there was no odour of other cats to attract at least Seymour, the clue or invitation we spoke of above. They could not possibly have belonged to the estate's previous owner because the Powells had been in place almost twenty years before cat number one fingered them. There was that, the picking of the Powells. Relatively easy was the conversion of the family. It had already been demonstrated they are an easy mark, although the cats could not possibly have known that until water and food dishes began appearing on the patio near the lemon tree. Even then, coming inside was a big step for Seymour to take.

But these cats are, as we shall see, the descendants of wild, solitary creatures, and society does not come easily or naturally to them. Many domestic cats simply cannot share a home with other cats. We have just found a home for one of our rescue cases, Clothilde. She despised having other cats around although she is a lovely animal in her own way. She needed and went to what would be a single-cat home on a nearby farm. Yet the Powell cats, masters at adaptation, obviously, snuggle up with each other to sleep, share food dishes, bathe each other, and sit around and watch each other play with stuffed mice and a myriad other toys. They have adjusted themselves perfectly to obtain and retain a luxurious lifestyle, not unlike that of the rich and famous.

There had to be a waiting and watching period with each of the three wanderers now on deck. Only the kitten Moca was a selection made by the human participants, but the others went shopping for people, found them, converted them, and made their oh so feline deal—beauty, love,

and tranquillity in exchange for a world of unending luxury and devotion. Cats play for high stakes, and the Powells have bought the package. All of this displays not only feline intelligence and adaptability but the cat's power to wait, watch, and select. Selectivity without observation is the wildest of wild gambling chances. Too often with cats it has been pick right or die.

Jill and I were recently house guests in the feline manor in Brentwood, and the morning we left for the airport I called to Jane from the drive: "Arby is out here in the bushes."

"No she's not. She's right here eating."

But there was a big marmalade cat out there, back in the bushes, just sitting and watching and, I am sure, waiting. The Powells don't stand a chance.

11

Music could be an interesting avenue of insight into a cat's view of the world, if we could understand how they relate to music. As far as I know, though, we don't—understand, that is, and they don't relate. It is worth thinking about for a moment or two, however. The only thing we seem to understand is that no cat likes any music when it is too loud. As with human hearing, cats are always on the threshold of pain. You don't have to go very far up in the decibel climb before any sound, even music, even Mozart, is sheer agony. If you take sound up too far for cat or man, you cause great stress, give ulcers, impair normal brain patterns, alter behaviour, make concentration impossible, and, at a level that is surprisingly easy to achieve, you can kill. Cats get to all of these points except possibly the very last sooner than we do, apparently, because they plug into the sound before we do, at much lower levels of amplification and frequency.

Some cats seem to hate all music, or at least they absent themselves the moment the stereo or radio is turned on, or when there is too much of it between gunshots and canned laughter on television. Whether that is due to conditioning, hypersensitivity, or the cat's naturally critical make-up is not easy to determine. Cats are, we know, very critical of a great many things they encounter in their lives. That is one of the greater feline paradoxes; once they accept an individual or the members of a household, they can be doglike, they are so non-judgemental. But when it comes to strangers, human or animal, food, and all of the elements that make up their lives, they can be very hard to please. Why cats were given such terrific peripheral vision when they spend so much of their time looking down their noses is difficult to understand.

There are cats that seem to be indifferent to music, or at least it doesn't cause them to stir as long as it stays away from disturbing levels. Whether they are being cool about it, playing life with a poker face, and are really thrilled to death by *Finlandia* or the *1812 Overture* is not easy to determine. I have watched sleeping cats that have not so much as wiggled a whisker when the music came on, but if it is turned up too high they simply get up and leave the room. If you listen carefully, you will hear cats in that kind of a situation muttering to themselves. If we ever find out how to translate a cat's vocal offerings, I am absolutely certain we will learn that they swear, a lot.

Then there are cats that appear to like music (tagging a cat as a music *lover* would seem to take things a bit far). Several years ago I did a television show about cats in their places living their varied lifestyles and we took our cameras to an apartment in Greenwich Village, where a young composer lived with his wife and their six cats. One of the cats planted himself on top of the piano as soon as the young fellow sat down to play or compose. The cat, as I recall, was a smoky Persian, and he leaned over and watched his owner's hands on the keyboard with his own front paws drooping over the edge. After a few minutes he would rearrange himself on a pile of music manuscript sheets and either sleep or sit with a glassy, contented look on his handsome face. He had something private going on, no doubt about it.

And indeed there was an added factor there. A grand piano, baby to concert, has anywhere from fifty to eighty tons of pull on its harp when the instrument is properly tuned, as I recall. When the padded hammers hit such extremely taut strings, you get vibrations, which is, of course, what we hear, those of us not in contact with the instrument. Inside the box, though, those vibrations are even more intense. For a sensitive animal to be in intimate contact with the box with perhaps a fifth or sixth of its total body surface must be a stirring experience. Music under those conditions would be felt as a tingling caress almost as much as it would be heard. That same thing, approximately, can be achieved by turning really heavy-duty stereo speakers up high, but there is that deterrent, it hurts that way. Lying on a piano that is being played in a moderate fashion would give you a very pleasing tactile sensation without drilling a hole through your head. A music-enjoying cat should find the top of a piano really quite rewarding. I have seen other cats using a piano top that way, for a massage, apparently.

It would be interesting to determine if cats have tastes in music. They do in everything else, unrelentingly. One supposes that a music-enjoying cat that lived in the home of Isaac Stern, Pinchas Zuckerman, or Yitzhak Perlman might pick up on Mozart before it did on the Rolling Stones, while a cat that lived with a rock buff might even prefer acid or punk rock to Grofé, Verdi, or Tchaikovsky. It might all be a matter of conditioning, but it could be individual taste, one supposes.

In some of our earlier speculations we moved down an imaginary trail through the sizes of matter until we passed the nucleus of the atom and got into subatomic particles. By going further, we decided we would leave matter behind altogether and reach the point where it was all energy, some of it harmonics, and wondered if that world, the cosmos, in fact, wasn't really all music that like a jelly mould finally settles into something with at least a degree of firmness. (The planet we live on is apparently no firmer than a jelly mould, what with shifting tectonic plates and all, so the analogy would seem credible enough.) Could music, harmonics and all, have special meanings for cats and their sensitive sensory array?

All of this is somewhat vague, I'll own, but, then, so is our grasp on the mechanics of our own awareness. The harmonics that can gel into matter, anything from cats to continents, probably could not be assigned to any musical genre (except, perhaps, the sounds of the heavenly hosts—a lot of strings, I imagine), but the way cats might relate to sound, vibrations from the shrill to the thunderous, would transcend all that. Perhaps there is something to the idea of climbing to the top of a high hill on a clear evening with your cat in your arms and listening together to the sounds of the stars. But we are matter ourselves and so we are made up of molecules with nuclei and atoms, so in a very real sense we should be able to stand cat-in-arms listening to ourselves. Perhaps that is exactly what cats are doing when they get that very faraway look in their eyes, listening to an inner music, an inner truth. A cat's body, after all, contains about 4 million million cells. A single drop of a cat's blood may contain between 3 and 4 million blood cells. A lot of particles are whirring around at wild, wild speeds, and in each of those particles are the submatter pulses of energy we might call matter music. It is a very impressive inner orchestra.

None of this gets really spooky unless we ask the question, can cats hear our constructive music, too? Somewhere there are extrasensory capabilities that explain how cats function. It is clear that five to five-and-a-half senses just don't cover it. If it is the micro-harmonics of creation playing for our cats' benefit, we are into something here we have never dealt with before, extrasensory perception on a perfectly grand scale.

If cats operate on such titanic scales of perception and are locked into their (our!) cosmos in such an inextricable way, then it may have been Lewis Carroll whose perception of the cat was not only most whimsical and lyrical but perhaps closest to the truth of the beast:

> "All right," said the Cat; and this time it vanished quite slowly, beginning with the end of the tail, and ending with the grin, which remained some time after the rest of it had gone.

Somehow I like the concept that a cat that is watching me is grinning. That suggests a superior knowledge of some kind, or at least a different and very good drummer. I want to believe that something like that is true of my cats. (Carroll's view of the lingering grin was probably based on a cheese made in Cheshire whose hallmark is a cat's head with a grin on its face. The rest of the cat is not shown in this very old logo.)

12

Although it surely does not affect the way cats see us (as would be the case if they wore the rose-coloured glasses that get so many of us through life), it is an interesting rider to note that cats watch us through a far wider range of eye colours than we do them. They outdo dogs in this regard as well. In fact, I can't think of one domestic animal that comes close to them in this particular form of splendour. Since we don't selective-breed (genetically manipulate) wild species, there are probably no wild animals including the wildcat species that match them, either. Purebred cats are bred for eye colour as they are for so many other preferred breed points or standards. It is a matter of human taste that dictates all of this. The gene potential for eye-colour flexibility has had to be there all along, however, and one must wonder why. Under what circumstances can blue eyes have a survival advantage over green or hazel? Coloration in the animal kingdom serves to hide the animal, or at least help it to be as invisible as possible, and like flags and name tags colour also serves to help animals of one species identify each other when it is time to breed. Eye colour in cats would not seem to serve either of these purposes. We do not know that seeing through one colour of eye is in any way better than seeing through another.

Try as we might, project as we will, we can't see people or objects as other people see them. Even with our wonderful powers of description, we will always be limited to the assumption that our eye colours have nothing whatsoever to do with how we see the world around us, only how others see us. We must assume that is the case with cats as well. It is likely to be a long time before scientists figure out how we can see with cats' eyes. They do have a remarkable variety of colours, though, and that does add to the inherent mystery of the beast, not to mention its great beauty and undeniable individuality.

All kittens start out with blue eyes. It is not until they are several weeks old that the blue begins to show signs of adulteration and adult colours begin to settle in. The ever popular Siamese and the less well-known Himalayans retain the blue and in fact it can intensify as an animal approaches maturity. Some white cats, both long- and short-hair varieties, also retain their baby blue eye colour, but unfortunately the gene that gives a cat white fur and blue eyes carries a recessive characteristic for deafness. An awful lot of cats with those colours are born with no hearing at all and no potential for it as they grow older. We had a cat like that and he was not only deaf but retarded. (The latter problem may have come about as the result of repeated collisions with our massive bulldog, Pudge. Pudge would get up a full head of steam and begin running with the grace of a bulldozer. On a number of occasions Mr. Amanda got in the way and was literally knocked unconscious. The poor dear was never the same after that. Eventually Pudge had to go and live with friends who raised bears and mountain lions. She was better matched.) Anyway, Mr. Amanda had the bluest of blue eyes set far apart in the whitest of white faces and both were as blank as freshly painted barn walls. He once caught his tail on fire when he got too near a candle and the expression on his face never changed. The house smelled for days and Mr. Amanda would peer at his tail from time to time with a puzzled look on his face. The other animals would have nothing to do with him. Having him in the room was like attending a wig barbecue.

Persians are the only cats that can have true copper eyes, and breeders work furiously to keep that remarkable colour in their line. White Persians, though, are desirable with blue eyes (but good hearing) or odd eyes—one eye blue and the other brown, copper, or some other colour. Silver Persians are highly prized with green eyes. One breed of cat, we should marvel, has the eye-colour range of blue-copper-green. And they can be littermates.

Burmese cats have yellow or gold eyes and they can be quite awesome, especially if you try to stare such a creature down. Abyssinians have eyes that range from gold through green to hazel. Russian and British blues can have the most brilliantly green eyes of all; they can be true emerald. Korats and Havana Browns have chartreuse eyes at best, although yellow-green is common and not too shabby in a cigar brown animal.

The multicolour breeds and random-bred cats have even more latitude.

Ideally, their eye colours will conform somewhat to coat colours in what should be a kind of designer-approved harmony. Reddish cats should have gold eyes, silver tabbies appear to be at their best with green eyes, and white cats can have that tricky blue eye colour or gold or be odd-eyed. Those eye colours have an optimum period in the young adult cat and may weaken as the animal ages or if it breeds very often. Altering a cat or spaying it *can* also weaken eye colour, but whether that is due to a change in hormones or simply the shock of anaesthesia and other bodily insults is not known. Wouldn't it be just like a cat to get even with you for having it castrated by changing its gorgeous eye colour!

We started with the disclaimer that this brief discussion of eye colour is a rider, albeit a logical one in a book about cats watching us. There doesn't appear to be any particular logic to it all, but cats are like that, as we all know, full of little nooks and crannies where secrets may hide. Since it is known that blue eyes in a cat carry a weakness—the tendency towards deafness—may we assume other eye colours, perhaps on their own or perhaps linked to certain overall pigments, carry strengths and weaknesses? We have no evidence that that is so, and as is the case with so many other things about cats it is cause for wonder, something to think about. Keep in mind when we hold that blue-eyed white cat up for consideration that white is not the lack of colour. Quite the opposite is true. Black is the absence of colour; white is the presence of all colours at the same time. So when we see a white cat, we are seeing an intensely coloured animal, an animal that is perhaps colour-saturated. Now add blue eyes and you can probably subtract hearing. How little we know about what happens beyond the tips of the whiskers as we move in towards the animal itself.

As recently as twenty-five or thirty years ago if you raised the question of cognition, if you asked whether cats *thought*, you would have been considered a card-carrying nut. Scientists, by far the vast majority of them at least, would have been merciless in their condemnation of your silliness or, as the cardinal sin of zoology was then known, anthropomorphism. Sneering was in, and was considered good form for anyone with a graduate degree. It was all so neat in those days. Human beings as creatures were distinguished by several absolutely irrefutable facts: human beings thought, animals didn't, no arguments allowed; human beings had language, animals didn't, period; human beings alone were tool-using, like it or not. It was all summed up neatly in the concept that human beings alone, not animals, had culture.

The ultimate absurdity rests in that latter concept. Culture refers to things that are only man-made, material, spiritual, and intellectual, and it is obviously true that animals do not do or make man-made things. Why in heaven's name would they want to? They don't need them. As for the other distinguishing characteristics, no longer so quick and easy. I have watched one of our dogs drag a box to a gate and stand on it to get over the obstruction. Some birds and certainly chimpanzees not only use tools, they manufacture them. There are miles of film and videotape showing chimpanzees at Jane Goodall's research station at Gombe on Lake Tanganyika in Tanzania selecting a twig, stripping it of leaves, licking it to cover it with saliva, then inserting it into a hole in an ants' nest. Withdrawing the twig now covered with ants, they licked it clean. Certain vultures faced with the armoured reality of an ostrich egg pick up stones and forcefully hurl them down on the egg again and again until the shell cracks and they can gain access to the treasure inside. Using a rock as a missile with a specific purpose in mind is technically somewhat different from launching a ballistic missile, but not as different as it might make us comfortable to think. A chimpanzee faced with a world of tasty ants just out of reach that picks a twig (selection of the proper raw material for toolmaking), strips it of leaves (readies it for a specific use), and then covers it with saliva (arms or fuels it) is not really all that different from a carpenter, a plumber, or a surgeon. We might feel safer on our pedestal if it were very, very different but such is simply not the case. (The chimpanzee's genetic package differs from our own by less than 1 per cent. They differ from gorillas by 13 per cent, but are almost identical to us, or we to them.)

Language? Whales have language. No one really doubts that any longer, and complex languages they are, too. Chimpanzees and gorillas that have been taught sign language "talk" to us with ease. Animals don't lack a language, as comforting to some people as it would be if it were only true, they lack the appropriate muscles and the experience to communicate in the ways we do. Our claim to the exclusive use of language has fallen by the way over the past two or three decades like a lot of other nonsense that used to masquerade as science. For some egocentrics it has been an unsettling time. For people really tuned in to animals it has been the era of the great big "I told you so". And no one I know can be smugger than cat owners, particularly if they feel their friends have been maligned. Perhaps that is not quite right. When it comes to smugness, cats generally outdo cat owners by a handsome margin. That is why the two understand each other so well. They get satisfaction from the same kinds of things.

I cannot think of a case of tool-using in cats, at least I have witnessed no such episodes. But cats are very vocal when they are upset or feeling deprived (ever try delaying a cat's meal by an hour or so?), and they have no trouble at all making us understand what stinkers we are being. I don't know whether purring qualifies as communication or what else in the way of vocalisation they do that legitimately falls into that category, but I am sure there are other forms. But before going on to speculate further on the subject of other feline senses, other means which they may use to interpret the world they live in, let's attack that last of the old maxims we were raised on, the silly one about animals not *thinking*.

Quietly, over the last quarter of a century or so, books have begun appearing—largely targeted for graduate students studying psychology and animal behaviour and related disciplines—which deal with comparative cognition. I attended an international conference in Massachusetts in 1987 where scientists had gathered not to wonder *if* animals think but rather how they think and what they might think about. Times have changed. Animal cognition is now a legitimate subject for consideration. Animals apparently do think. Since cats are carnivores, rather high-on-the-scale mammals, they would have to qualify if anything does below the apes and whales. We can now say with a fair degree of certainty (absolute certainty in my mind) that cats think. That, surely, is worth consideration since they probably think about what they are seeing or hearing, and very often that is us.

It would seem highly unlikely that cats think the way we do, although we can't really define the way we think. It would be a pretty unprofitable pursuit to try to understand how cats think. Since that is in the realm of 100 per cent speculation we might just set it aside and consider the matter from other angles.

We know that even in times of repose, information pours as if from a hose into the cat's brain in quantities far, far beyond the cat's ability to analyse. Somehow a small quantity—perhaps seven to ten bits out of every ten thousand every conscious second—is singled out and used to cue the cat's immediate response patterns. How that selection is made is not known, but there is inevitably all that data left over. It is unlikely that it is stored or kept as a backlog for later consideration. Since the incoming data are continuous, that backlog would become a totally hopeless logjam in less than one minute. In one normal feline day, the cat would have had to store more bits of information unused than it could utilise at the normal rate of its entire lifetime. The other fact we have already considered is that most of it would be useless seconds after it was received since it would deal with immediate and highly transient phenomena.

A scenario: A dog the cat has never seen before and will possibly never see again suddenly leaps the fence into the cat's territory, runs across the garden, jumps another fence, is gone. It is a simple enough episode in the life of a cat, the kind of all-of-a-sudden thing that happens to it hundreds or perhaps thousands of times during its life. In a state of considerable agitation the cat takes signals at a rate perhaps far greater than ten thousand per second. It would be rather like a radiation detector passing over a hot spot. The *beep-beep-beep* rate would shoot up and then drop off. Once the dog is gone, what is the cat going to do with all that information? Besides the tiny number of data already selected and put to use in some appropriate survival tactic, what good is all the rest? To clutter up the storage capacity of its brain would not only be useless but counterproductive, for clutter it would be, and clutter in your attic or your skull compounds itself until finding anything becomes an almost impossible task.

The scenario of the incoming/outgoing dog, however, might not be useless if absorbed in some way other than as random data bits hooked to the single transient incident. Cats, we know, learn from almost the moment of birth. Perhaps the cat somehow selects the seven to ten bits of information out of ten thousand in order to supply instant reflexive reaction should it be needed to avoid hazard and scans the rest to create a learning experience in a very much compressed format. From our simple scenario, a cat could learn that the fence around its garden is not as secure a device as it was perhaps originally perceived to be. A dog can jump over it. Dogs are different from cats in that a cat faced with that fence would have first jumped up onto it and then down the other side. Rarely would a cat risk jumping over a fence without knowing what is in or near the landing zone. Fact: dogs can jump into your garden. Fact: dogs are less cautious than cats in most instances. Fact: a dog can race across your garden on its own mission (which you can fail to interpret) and then jump out of the garden. The fact that the dog did not instantly attack the cat instead of continuing on its mission could teach the cat something about that dog should it ever encounter it again.

Also, if you sense by smell or hearing (or what else?) an animal outside your fence, you might automatically scan the fence top where the animal would be likely to land if it is a cat, and have an opportunity to put on enough of a threat display to discourage the cat from leaping down into

your garden. But you will almost surely not have that time and space buffer if it is a dog. If the dog is thinking about coming into your garden it will happen very, very quickly and you had better have something more practical up your paw than a threat display. A minor fact: a dog on a mission can ignore you but just might not if you did put on a challenging threat display. In a word, let leaping dogs keep right on leaping.

All of that (and perhaps a great deal more, if you have a cat's view of life and leaping dogs) could be learned from even that simple hypothetical episode in a suburban back garden. *Does the cat think about it as it learns from it*, and does the stuff of learning for long-range use come from the data that is left over after instantaneous reflexes are ordered up by central control? Probably yes to the latter question. The first must give us some pause.

The next time you notice a cat fixing you with that enigmatic stare with eyes that are blue, green, chartreuse, gold, copper, yellow, brown, or whatever else may have come genetically forward in the animal's line, remember the cat is not just seeing you, it is not just recording you. It is contemplating you, evaluating you, and not just as an individual for the moment at hand but rather as part of its long-range store of information about the human race. Cats probably use data entering through their battery of senses in long form and short form. Examples of each: *"Let's work around near the toolshed. It was loaded with voles yesterday and we ate ourselves into a coma."* That would be long form. Short form? *"Let's get the hell out of here, that lorry isn't slowing down!"*

How sophisticated thinking in cats may be can't even really be the subject of serious speculation. They certainly draw on experience in the long form (in the truly short form there wouldn't be time to think—even we don't begin thinking about it until after we have reflexively dropped the red-hot poker) and they have the mix of genetically imparted species wisdom to put to work as well. Although we may be light-years away from truly understanding it, we can appreciate the fact that some form of cognitive capability is there.

13

Even as this manuscript progresses, affairs of the cat progress here at Thistle Hill. Since our earlier discussion of the Thistle Hill Regulars, the somewhat spooky barn cats we inherited, a palomino Arab mare has arrived who is destined to become our foundation brood mare. We are planning her first assignation now. She broke a leg some time back and although she is now reasonably sound again it is too expensive for most people without their own farm to keep a horse they can't ride. In some areas it can cost between $800 and $1200 a month to board a single horse. Since Sherry shouldn't jump any more and shouldn't be ridden heavily by an adult or on rough ground, she needed a home. She got it at Thistle Hill. She is only seven years old and is as gentle as she can be. The cats appear to be comfortable around her and she with them. But cats and horses have traditionally got on exceptionally well. High-strung racehorses are often given a cat as a companion to travel with so no stall or van is ever really foreign to them. Horses find cats reassuring. Cats find that horses as grain eaters are likely to attract rodents.

A few days before Sherry came up from Virginia, a young and somewhat miniaturised Hereford steer came on campus and, unfortunately, has been named Steakums by my son-in-law. He is a pet and most certainly will never become steak. He lived a sad life in a horrible commercial petting zoo and had to be confiscated by humane authorities when he was found to be malnourished and dehydrated. It isn't easy to find a good home for a steer, even a sweet animal like this one. Steakums and Sherry the beautiful golden mare are now a herd unto themselves. It is nice seeing them out in their pasture together. Once Steakums learns that Sherry means it when she tells him she wants him for a friend only, it should be very peaceful. What a castrated bull thinks he sees in a female horse, even a pretty one, is beyond me, but a lot of things that happen between the ears of animals are beyond me.

A very elegant greyhound named Reggie, fresh off the track in Massachusetts and destined to be killed as fifty thousand greyhounds a year are killed as soon as they stop winning, has also been rescued and is now in our pack as well. It never stops. The same week Reggie joined the staff, the week after Sherry did, a friend of ours developed an allergy and needed a home for her two one-year-old seal-point Siamese girls. They are so attached to each other that they had to go as a unit. You guessed it, they did. Trouble and Jones are now Caras cats, too (renamed Elvira and Vampira). Some day we are going to have to stop doing this.

The coming of Sherry and Steakums means my wife and I spend much more time in and around the barn than we did before. It isn't a case of hour after hour but it does mean several visits a day. Chores involving a shovel and pitchfork are inevitable, and there are grain, hay, and water to be seen to, not to mention a little good old-fashioned socialising time. We want all of our animals to be gentle and used to human contact. That is just good conditioning whether you are dealing with cats or cattle, so we pat a lot and hand-feed carrots, and our steer and our horse now follow us like, well, barn cats. This all means we are seeing much more of the Thistle Hill Regulars close up. They are keenly interested both in the new animals and in us. Just three days ago, the Regulars began showing up on our porch, much to our surprise. They have taken to following us down the hill from the barn. They appear to be much less shy and, miracle of miracles, only this morning I patted one, apparently the mother, the largest of the white and brindled jobs. The all-black cat spat at me, but the bravado show didn't carry very much conviction. As my ancient English grandmother-in-law used to mutter when she had said something absurdly polite or polite but absurd, "Well, it was something to say."

Here is another case where we were studied with great care, apparently nearly twenty-four hours a day. Once again we can't imagine what kinds of notes were being taken or how the Regulars' opinions were shaped, but those cats have come round and are now clearly in an accepting mode. We are about to be labelled okay. Interestingly enough, they are all coming round together. It is too much to think of that fact as coincidence. Not at all. It is a concerted move, a change in attitude based on their

Drawing by Steinlen

observations. Again, pooled information or impressions?

It was more than curiosity that kept the Regulars on patrol, it was an effort to learn something, to figure something out. They had questions they needed answers for before carrying out some plan. Surely some manner of thinking was involved as the Regulars not only watched but studied us. At some point, obviously, something tipped the scales and the total of what had been observed came up positive. Cats that are looking for a better lifestyle study their subjects with a peculiar intensity. It is obvious that a great deal is at stake. They watch so that they can be equipped to make judgements and come to decisions. It all has real purpose. We have no intention of making them house cats, we have enough of those, but we will see what happens when the weather turns bad.

Our observations of cats as observers themselves is not a new phenomenon in the human-animal relationship. Cats were exported from Egypt to Italy at least as far back as the fifth century B.C. That is when they are first found there in Greek art. Very often the intensity of the cat as a watcher is a featured, if not the main, subject of the work. On one vase—a *kotyle* from Apulia dating to approximately 400 B.C.—a naked youth, probably representing the city's founder, stands with a tiny bird held above his head in his right hand. He has a small cat clinging to his back and it is studying the bird with that fierce intensity only a cat can muster, a paw raised to strike out at the first opportunity. From about the same time another vase—this time a *lekane*—manufactured in Campania (a Greek province between Rome and Naples) shows two women, one draped, the other naked, watching a cat that once again is fiercely intent on a bird the naked woman is holding aloft. Whether these scenes, almost certainly drawn from real life, mean that the Greek settlers in Italy liked to tease cats and then feed them live birds, or whether the sheer magnetism of watching the cat watching was some form of recreation or symbolism is not clear. But, long ago, cats were watching, and it was interesting enough to human observers to turn the episodes into pieces of eternally fascinating art.

The theme continued into Roman times. In a museum in Naples there is a mosaic taken from Pompeii during its excavation. In the centre is a high pedestal on which stands an ornamental bowl with parrots and a dove perched on its rim. To the right, a cat crouches, with huge round eyes. It, too, has a paw raised for the death blow although the birds are clearly out of reach. The same motif appears again and again in art from all over the world, the intensity of a cat studying its prey or almost anything else including human beings. The motif is seen repeatedly in Japanese paintings. Try to remember how many photographs you have seen taken in Paris and Rome that show cats sitting in a window, on a sill, or a doorstep simply watching the parade of city life flow past. We have watched cats watching us and everything else, apparently, as long as we have had domestic cats, something in the order of four thousand years.

Going back to Pompeii. Interestingly enough there are only a few odd scraps in the ruins to show that there were cats in that poor, bedevilled city before Vesuvius orchestrated its catastrophic end. Yet we are reasonably certain there were cats up to that time. There is the mural now in Naples, and the fact that every other Roman city we know anything about had cats galore. Where were the Pompeiian cats on that fateful day? It is entirely likely that the cats' sensory array enables them to anticipate geothermal upheavals as well as seismic disturbances. This presumed ability has been attributed to their sensitivity to vibrations (which certainly start far below where we could sense them), to high-pitched sounds as gases escaped from the earth where they had been building up under enormous pressure (the sound of that gas, at least in the early phases, would be at a pitch much higher than we could detect), and to a possible shift in the earth's magnetic fields. Any or all of these things could be clues for a cat to get out of town. Note that only one of those suggestions, geomagnetism, depends on anything outside the standard sensory package.

There was a story and I can't remember where I read it (it was a long time ago) about a man with two cats in San Francisco at the time of the great earthquake. For a day or so before the first shock hit, his cats carried on in obvious nervous despair. He finally locked them in a room when they became intolerable with their wailing and pacing. He was not at home when the quake hit and when he at last managed to fight his way through the rubble, the confusion, and the rescue parties, he found his house totally destroyed. He assumed his cats had died as the building collapsed and burned. He suffered great guilt for not having "listened" to his friends. Two days later, as he was picking through the rubble, one of his cats appeared. An hour later, he found the second one. How they survived is anyone's guess, but what is important is that they had the sensory acuity, or at least it so seems, to predict or anticipate the impending tragedy. That speaks to the cats' senses, surely.

Whether such anecdotes are true or apocryphal is impossible to say. They make a point either way: most people are not satisfied with five-sense cats. They expect something beyond, and certainly anything beyond could very well include being able to foretell an impending cataclysm.

Some clues as to just how intelligent, sensitive, and *individualistic* cats are can be found by observing them in their daily lives. Referring again to the Thistle Hill Regulars, they were, we know, denied human companionship as kittens. An unknown tom, a "travelling man", came through one day, and the queen who was herself born here only eight months earlier was put in the family way. Some time between sixty-one and seventy days later the offspring we see here now (they are about full-grown) appeared in a secret tunnel among bales of hay in the barn. We have since found the nest.

The owners of the farm were hardly animal lovers and the kittens were not given shots, were probably not even seen until they were out in the open hunting rats and mice and songbirds on their own. They were totally unsocialised. That kind of a start can make almost any cat impossible to deal with by the time it is four to five months old. Unsocialised cats are usually terrified of people and certainly unresponsive to overtures of affection. But not the Thistle Hill Regulars. Their mother was un-socialised as well, so there was nothing to learn from her that could be positive in a human-cat relationship, yet the lot of them are moving closer

every day to becoming pet cats. They are doing it on their own, without coercion. The fact that they will stand still and allow themselves to be touched is astounding. Nothing could better demonstrate just how individualistic the cat is. Why these cats are moving in this direction, towards relationships with human beings, when every rule says they should be doing just the opposite since we are strangers on their land, is difficult to understand except for the fact that these cats obviously did a great deal of homework before coming to their decision. The real mystery is how or why they are all doing it at the same time at about the same speed. I just can't believe they sat around and had a conference. But whatever is going on adds up to intelligence, the incorporation of first-hand observations that were so intense and so acute they could overcome natural and generally justifiable fear. Wild kittens born to a wild-born mother just don't walk up and get themselves petted, and they don't follow people around all day making notes. But they do here at Thistle Hill.

We can go to cats we don't know, any young cats in fact, and watch play behaviour. Watch a kitten or young cat stalk a bit of fluff, move around it, lay a trap for it, and then pounce for the kill. That cat knows it isn't chasing a mouse. The object of the mock attack is failing to give off all kinds of real mouse signals, and yet the cat is turning the inanimate material into a make-believe mouse, it is using its imagination (whatever that really is in cats). Make-believe or "pretend", as my granddaughter calls it, takes intelligence, and we often judge the progress of children by how imaginative they are, how inventive. Cats are enormously inventive when it comes to turning each other or all kinds of passive objects and material into enemies and prey. They turn their entire world into one big educational toy.

Two cats rearing and swatting at each other, making mock attacks, are creating in their play a make-believe life situation and are both enjoying themselves and learning from their efforts. And it is good exercise. The

Drawings by Steinlen

fact that the cats in play battles frequently change roles—one the aggressor one minute and the other the next—shows that they are not serious. Play behaviour is a yardstick of intelligence, and the range of imaginary objects and situations used in play an even more refined measurement. Cats rank very high on both scales. The incoming sensory deluge pouring its signals into a cat's brain triggers marching orders in a highly developed, wonderfully sharp, and truly creative organ. Anyone who doubts this probably has not spent much time watching cats.

On the subject of watching cats, a not-so-minor footnote. Staring is not rude in the world of the cat, it is hostile, and can be terrifying. We forget too often, I think, how intimidating we must be to an animal that probably weighs on the average under ten pounds. Fixing a cat with an intense stare can easily be interpreted by the animal as threatening and dangerous. Try to watch cats when you are not likely to make repeated or prolonged eye contact. It is true that cats study us, but seldom by looking directly into our eyes. Watch your cat, don't stare it down. You don't have to prove to your cat that you are bigger and stronger than it is; your cat already knows, probably better than you do. The better your manners from the cat's point of view, the more you will see, and the better you will come to understand the nature of the beast you are dealing with. To call the orderly behaviour of cats "manners", of course, is a slight liberty taken with the language; but when you watch cats long enough, it does appear as if they do have a behaviour code that approaches social nicety. Sometimes even the most outrageously anthropormorphic language can help understanding as long as everyone involved maintains reasonable perspective.

14

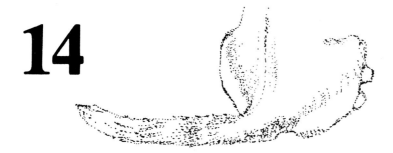

Cats have had rather a better image in countries steeped in mystery and what it pleases us of the Western world to call superstition. For reasons we don't fully understand, the cat is never mentioned in the Bible, not once, although an awful lot of other animals are. That could be because much of the Bible comes from manuscript material recorded not long after the cat was first domesticated. Dogs had already been around for between ten and twenty thousand years and so get talked about. The cat was rather new to the human collection of living artefacts. That is the most likely answer I have been able to come up with.

Perhaps as a result of its absence from the ``Good Book´´, the Judaeo-Christian world has treated cats with almost insane ambivalence. Sacred one minute, profane the next, that is the way it has gone. Coddled, spoiled, adored, then tortured hideously and blamed for all the ills of the world. Loving pet on Tuesday, the familiar of witches on Wednesday, and something in between for the weekend. One of my favourite characters in history was the admittedly bitchy but always fascinating Elizabeth I. I have always been saddened by her extreme cruelty to cats and the horrible way cats were treated in her time. She was powerful enough, feared enough, to have put a stop to it by example if not by fiat. She once had a large model of the Pope made of straw and basketry and then filled to the point of suffocation with live cats. She personally set it on fire. I am in no way inclined to forgive her for that. It hasn't helped her image a bit. No doubt about it, she was her father's daughter. The big, hard-riding redhead was frequently monstrous, too, very quick with the torch. If the Catholics in the British Isles (and Ireland) want to do that to Protestants and the Protestants to Catholics, that is their business, but why cats? You can't hang original sin on cats, but they have come in for an awful lot of other baseless accusations.

Generally, cats had a better hand dealt to them in Asia. The Muslim world, somewhat surprisingly since the Muslims despise all dogs except the Saluki, has had a pretty decent attitude towards cats compared to Europe. The Prophet himself had a beloved cat he called Muezza, a nice Arabic name. They say he once wanted to stand up and go somewhere but noticed Muezza sleeping on the voluminous sleeve of his robe. Rather than disturb his feline friend, Mohammed cut the sleeve off and then stood up and walked away. There may have been a special symbolism there, the details of which are lost on us without the benefit of the full context. Slashing one's clothing in time of grief and other heavy emotional scenes is big with the Semites. That could have something to do with Mohammed's actions while Muezza slept. On another occasion, Mohammed saw his cat drinking from a water source and went to it to use the water to purify himself. That was more than affection, that was respect of a high order.

In Thailand, of course, their beautiful cats have long been highly prized and special ones have been kept in temples as sort of walking sacred relics. The Buddhists, a particularly sane group of philosophically inclined people for the most part, believed that the souls of people who had attained a high plateau of spirituality entered the bodies of cats when the people died and resided there until the cats were gathered, too. At that point, the souls of the saintly entered Paradise. Having an intermediate host is a fairly sophisticated concept, rather like the malaria organism taking up with a mosquito between human victims.

The Birman cat of Thailand is said to be the direct descendant of sacred temple cats of the Middle Ages, and the story has it that its gold fur and very blue eyes date to the death of the saintlike Lama Mun-Ha (a man who has failed to become a household name among us), and that seven days later the cat died, releasing Mun-Ha for his walk among the saints and other good folks in Paradise. The Birman's splendid raiments were apparently a reward for safeguarding Mun-Ha's soul during that critical intermediate week. The Birman's willingness to die so quickly so that Mun-Ha could have that extra time in the great garden of eternity was to his favour as well. If you know many Birman owners, you know the cats are getting a little of their own back. The fact that many Siamese cats have crossed eyes (we once had one whose eyes were so crossed I would get a headache just looking at her) dates to the time when one of that breed

Drawing by Awashima Chingaku

stared so long and so hard at Buddha's golden goblet that its eyes went all silly. Again, the intently watching cat. The darkish mark on the back of a Siamese cat's neck, the so-called temple mark, is a relic of the times when a god actually stooped and picked a cat up. When cats were brought to Japan by Chinese merchants in the tenth century A.D., their reputation rose even higher and they were treated with enormous affection and respect.

There is an interesting observation that can be made here about extrasensory powers, that is, anything beyond the big five. Anyone who has had the good fortune to spend a great deal of time in the land of Asia, as I have, knows the absolute faith even the most educated, sophisticated, and well-travelled people have in extrasensory powers among human beings. Nothing of any moment happens in Sri Lanka (formerly Ceylon), for example, without the state astrologer dictating the exact time for the conference or ceremony and even such details as what direction which people should be facing. To marry without an astrologer giving the exact schedule for the ceremony down to the minute would be considered impossible folly.

A brilliant and beautiful woman I knew by the name of Cynthia De Mel who was the wife of an ambassador, Vere De Mel, visited our home (then in New York), dined with me in London, and had me to their home in Colombo on numerous occasions. She graduated from an English university and did graduate work in the United States. Yet she told me the following story about how she got an heirloom diamond ring back. It had been hidden in a coffee tin under the bed of a part-time houseboy who had stolen it. When I asked her how she found out where to look, she said she had gone to the family seer and he had told her, describing the hapless youth down to the last detail although he had never seen him or even known of his existence. When I looked somewhat incredulous, which bordered, I must admit, on the rude, she just laughed and said we Westerners would never understand the powers of perception because we feared them and had to deny them because we couldn't explain them.

People like Cynthia who allow for amazing feats of perception and depth of comprehension among themselves, and especially in gifted individuals, see things in cats we don't seem to be able to see, and the presence of extra senses unnumbered is simply assumed. Such beliefs, which go as deep as religion itself and often meld with it, are taken as natural fact. Perhaps it is only in such a magical matrix that the cat can be understood at all. That is where cats belong.

Desmond Morris is on the other side in his book *Catlore* (1987) when he writes: "To start with, ESP is a contradiction in terms. Anything we perceive is, by definition, something that operates through one of our sense organs. So, if something is extrasensory, it cannot be perceived. Therefore there cannot be any such thing as ESP."

I can live with that, but we are not talking about things being *beyond* the cat's sense organs or modes. We are saying that we have not yet located and identified all of those organs or modes, and we have not taken into account the cat's power of cognition. Dr. Morris seems to be saying that he has identified all the ways in which cats can perceive. I doubt very much that that is true. As for the expression ESP, extrasensory perception, that is semantics. People use ESP, I believe, generally to mean any beyond the big five. NDSP would indeed be better than ESP—Newly Discovered Sensory Perception. I am terribly wary of scientists who want us to believe that everything that is to be known is already known, especially about things as perplexing, as confoundingly complex, as cats. That is simply not true now and it is extremely unlikely that it ever will be.

In the United States we spend about $2 billion a year on cat food, more than we do on baby food, we buy and our cats use over a million tons of cat litter every twelve months. Let us allow that the subjects of that much attention and fiscal stimulation have secrets, and NDSP is the way of the future. ESP is an inaccurate semantic quirk and conveys not scientific fact but profound wonder. Under no logical circumstances can the misuse of the term "extrasensory perception" negate the almost certainty that cats and perhaps humans, quite probably most animals, have some means of reaching out and gathering the data, the impressions, the reality of being that we have yet to get into our catalogue. And again the point: if there is even one extra means not presently listed as a sense, the gates are wide open. It just does not seem logical to say that there is only one more sense (not Dr. Morris's *extra* sense) when there could be a hundred.

It is the premise of this book that the five acknowledged senses constitute, in combination, a starting point only. Science and scientifically established "facts" can only ever be a starting point. The absolutes of science fall by the wayside at an incredible rate. If we did not believe, in fact if we did not know that there are always new facts and new points of view not only to supplement but to replace what is thought to be now known, there would be absolutely no point in having science at all. The role of science is not only to build on what we have already learned but to unlearn what we have erroneously thought we knew to be fact when it wasn't fact at all.

We know our cats imperfectly just as we know ourselves imperfectly, and one of the great mysteries we have yet to explain to the satisfaction of anyone who thinks with a fresh, clear, uncluttered mind is how cats draw the world into themselves and determine how they want to relate to it and to us.

In 1974, in Switzerland, there appeared an excellent book by Gillette

Grilhe called *The Cat and Man* that addresses a subject we have alluded to several times already—curiosity. In fact, without pondering on the how of it all, it sums the matter up very nicely:

> Curiosity is inborn. The cat is fascinated by his surroundings—even the smallest happening makes him eager for fresh adventures. New ground has to be explored in minute detail and every object examined; parcels are sniffed, as if the cat were trying to guess the contents; an unknown visitor is examined from head to foot to find out what he may be thinking, and if the answer is satisfactory, will be approached. The cat likes to watch you working and to know what you are doing.

I am not certain that cats examine strangers to determine what they are thinking, as Grilhe suggests, but if that were true it would indicate a truly profound power called mind reading. That enters into a realm where I, at least, feel lost. Such a power would have to presuppose telepathy, the projecting of brain waves, all kinds of wonderful things. I can't rule it out but it does slow one down because we know absolutely nothing about it except statistics, and, of course, show business where it has flourished for centuries. But the curiosity Grilhe speaks of is a certain sign of intelligence. The strange, remote cat in the forest near Seguin, Texas, was

Drawing by Steinlen

curious about us, the Thistle Hill Regulars are curious about us (to an apparent purpose), all the cats we have known in our lives have been that way, and stories come to mind about each of them. Anyone who doubts the curiosity of the cat (it doesn't kill them as often as it saves them) need only place a large empty paper bag or a cardboard box on the kitchen floor. In very short order the cat of the house will be in the container checking things out. An empty container of almost any kind draws a cat in as if it were a vacuum they absolutely had to fill.

Curiosity, like play, is a built-in characteristic, as Grilhe suggests. The large question is whether or not curiosity is casual and recreational. I think it is not. I think having fun is as serious as a matter can be. I think cats that are having fun are also gathering information to determine how the box or the bag can serve their purpose. Is there anything inside of value or interest? Does it have more than one way in and out? Does their sense of smell tell them that there has been something there before that they should know about? After all, good things like rats and mice can come back. Is the box a safe hiding place or a comfortable sleeping place? Does the container offer an advantageous view? Is it warm, something very important to cats? A cat that did not check out anything as intriguing as a big brown paper bag would have a poor attitude towards the world around him and could be in trouble at some future date because of it.

I don't think nature builds capabilities or behavioural imperatives into her creatures in random fashion. When we feel, or a cat feels, that investigation is a must or relaxation is a must, it is because they probably are. The cat has the greater wisdom of our two species because it pays attention to the calls it hears. We are the ones who have high blood pressure, ulcers, and heart attacks, not cats. We, for all our vaunted intelligence, and the potential is certainly there within us, also ignore our curiosity as we mature, at potentially a very high price to ourselves. Therein, by the way, lies a good part of the cat's appeal. Both kittens and kids start out life curious about absolutely everything. But we mature— we come to know more and more about less and less until finally we know practically everything about practically nothing. Then they give us a Ph.D. The cat retains many of its infantile characteristics (as do dogs) and that gives us the wonderful feeling of being needed long after our children are grown. If we could be as clever as the cat and not lose some of the more choice elements of childhood—like being curious and being able to unwind, play, and relax completely—not only would we be wiser in the end but the end would perhaps be slower in coming for most of us.

Grilhe comments on the fact that cats like to watch us work, and indeed that is true. I have a cat that likes to sit on the toilet lid and watch me shave and carry out my other rituals. Not far from here there is a new barn under construction and the several times I have driven by I have noticed the two carpenters up on the roofing beams hauling lumber up and pounding away with their hammers with admirable industry. Each time there has been a cat up there, too, watching like a foreman. Why cats watch so intently things that appear to have nothing to do with them or offer any opportunities to improve their lot may not be all that difficult to explain. First, cats may like us and enjoy being near us. It really could be that simple. Secondly, cats are in a strange in-between period in their evolution. they came to us not all that long ago as solitary animals. Of the feline tribe, of course, only lions are at all gregarious. We have taken a solitary creature into our homes and lives and insisted that they become gregarious, too, no matter what their normal inclinations may be. By enveloping a cat within our lives, mixing it in with other cats, dogs, and lots of people, we are manipulating this creature and as the years pass it is becoming something new. Just as our knowledge can never be complete, so is that true of our domesticated animals. They are changing almost constantly into something new because we are changing ourselves, altering the degree to which we depend on animals, changing our religious beliefs, and forcing the animals we hold hostage to take a lot of blame for things they could not possibly know anything about. There is a third factor: a cat doesn't know in advance what concerns it and what does not. That may be the single biggest element in curiosity in cats. *"Should I worry about this or can I afford to ignore it?"* It is, after all, a fairly important question for a cat or a human being to ask.

Drawing by Steinlen

15

Not every lesson a cat learns will have universal application during its entire lifetime, and the small bundle, as powerful and well-built as it is for its size—about 290 bones, with 517 muscles anchored to the skeleton, 30 teeth, excellent claws, powerful tendons, fine balance, extraordinary climbing ability (better going up, very often, than coming down) plus speed and wits—is surprisingly vulnerable. Cats somehow seem to understand this and to remain on the defensive much of the time. That understanding may be largely instinct, in fact, it would almost have to be. A lot of life's most critical lessons are learned first hand with just about an animal's last breath. A cat might have to die to learn it isn't all-powerful as it liked to think it was—if cats think that way. After all, if there weren't television, movies, magazines, and books, you might not know about guns. On the day you learned about them, you might die during the lesson because you were in the process of being used as a target. Dead people and dead cats don't pass along first-hand hazardous experiences as genetic information and they don't pass on lore. Some things have to be built in simply because they are useless when learned from experience. It may be tough for nature to build guns into our genes, but a general alertness, even wariness, is a natural part of a species' survival.

We spoke earlier of our smallest resident, Sumay, the baby Siamese cat. Sumay arrived on board in the middle of our move to Thistle Hill Farm, and a frantic time it was. Sumay did not get to meet all of the four-legged residents on staff at the same time. In the long run that was probably easier on his nerves. There was no stampede of dogs and cats coming at him but a controlled trickling. It also helped that the animals arriving were occupied with making themselves familiar with the new digs and gave Sumay less attention than they might otherwise have given to a novelty like a new kitten. In a period of weeks, as I reconstruct the era, Sumay had to meet Siafu the silver ash tabby, and the two Siamese who joined us about the same time, Jones and Trouble. There was Lizzie, the basset hound, Duncan the border collie, whose father, Mike, starred in *Down and Out in Beverly Hills,* and also the newly arrived greyhound, Reggie. Then our housekeeper in East Hampton began shuffling the other dogs down: bloodhounds like Jedidiah, Penny, Forrester, Mandy, and Colby, and the two petite basset griffon vendeen, Guy and Celeste. Friends often bring their animals when they arrive at our place as house guests and Christopher the marmalade cat, Benson the pointer, and Tee the bearded collie all came and went. Our daughter Pamela and her husband Joe (with daughter Sarah) live nearby and at various times Apollo and Stanley the greyhounds, Zack the Labrador retriever, Fontine the smooth collie, and Annie, a Jack Russell terrier, all came for the day or the day and the night. Friends spent the day with Ruffian the Norfolk terrier in tow. I think that's about it. Sumay, who probably didn't weigh much more than a pound to a pound and a half through that hectic period of introductions, had to weather it all.

Any animal on that roster of recent Thistle Hill visitors could have killed Sumay with a pounce or a snap. He had to evaluate every new encounter as if each were the first animal he had ever met. When he wasn't being carried for his own protection (against human feet more than other animals), he hid under things and stared in near disbelief from whatever hiding place he was using at the moment. He stopped spitting after the first day and now walks towards, around, and under the larger dogs and dwells among other cats with near-total indifference. The other cats he has met are peaceful and either ignore him or, in the case of Siafu, hug and bathe him endlessly. Siafu is an altered male and either is the most attentive big brother in the world or has his hormones careening around in confusion because he really does appear to be mothering Sumay.

So, with a bit of careful observation and plenty of reinforcement, Sumay has the present household taped. He has isolated potential threats (he is so small that Annie the Jack Russell has to be watched) and some of the dogs play rough-and-tumble games that it is best to avoid when you are outweighed forty to fifty to one. But the one big lesson is that dogs and cats can be friendly and are not necessarily hostile. Unfortunately, it can't

be depended upon. The next big tom or the next dog that comes along may be a hater and a killer, and Sumay, no matter how big he is when he is full-grown, must, like all cats, be constantly alert and therefore forever watchful.

Cats in their relationship to our species have much the same problem. Elizabeth I was not the only cat burner in history, Hitler, Napoleon, and Alexander not the only cat haters. The next human being Sumay encounters might try to crush his still tender skull or break his ever vulnerable back. Some nut may want to soak him in petrol or lighter fuel and set him on fire, or use him for target practice with anything from a b–b gun to an elephant gun. It has all happened to lots of cats before, and cats that have survived to breed have been the wariest cats on the block and have kept wariness moving forward with their genes. In fact, natural caution—call it spookiness if you wish—is about the most important behavioural trait an animal can pass along, after mating and parenting instincts.

When cats look long and hard and repeatedly at people and animals they know well it may be an act of affection, interest, or reassurance; they don't know that it is a well-honed defence mechanism. When you are being held as permanent hostages, as our cats are, when you are small, which the largest domestic cat is in comparison to people and big dogs, and when your quick, sinuous movements attract rough, ill-mannered attention, looking is living. I don't think we can assign too much in the way of conscious motivation to most of the things cats do, but if we could I should think that staying alive and well would be the principal motive for a cat's attention to the details of the world.

Calling cats cognitive on the one hand and suggesting their motives are not conscious on the other is not really a contradiction. It is one thing to be able to work something out and avoid immediate calamity, but quite another to deal with abstract facts and recognise long-range hazards. As suggested earlier, cats are a package of blessings—cognition to some degree, genetic programming, conditioning, excellent senses, those we know and those we almost certainly don't know, and lightninglike reflexes. Put all these elements together and add the intensity of a cat's powers of observation, the feline style of concentration, and you have an animal that has survived enormously hazardous times. Even as ratters and mousers they are the least economically significant of all man's mammalian friends. For that reason they have been afforded the least amount of protection and therefore have had to do the most for themselves.

There is an interesting irony in the fact that cats are masters at appearing to be independent and self-sufficient. That bit of hubris has

Drawing by Steinlen

created a very dangerous fiction. It is dangerous because a great many people believe what their cats are telling them and do not care for them or guard them against present hazard anywhere near as well as they should. That is not healthy for cats. The proud little hairballs, in fact, would be far better off if they would just admit their vulnerability and throw themselves on the mercy of the merciful among us. They are too proud for their own good. A little less strutting might lengthen feline life expectancy.

16

Our familiar domestic cat did not spring up out of the earth wholly made and unaffiliated. And we did not really create very much of this wondrous creature ourselves by gene manipulation at breeding time or the other meddling things we do that bring about domestication. The idea that we did, however, seems to please some people. I find that difficult to understand. Ego is fine in moderation; in fact, in our dealings with things like cats it is essential to our intellectual survival. But Olympian claims are something else. The cat family was surely here long before we were (they used to eat us when we first began emerging from ancient ancestral loins) and we have been able to do little more than clean up a few of the rough spots around the edges to achieve the little homebody with which we are concerned here. Much of what we found is a lot of what we've got. Wildness so genetically close to hand is surely one of the most fascinating things about our pets. I wonder what the self-proclaimed creators see in the cat, or what they really want from it that they are moved to claim authorship. I take far more joy in knowing a little of the wild part of the story, a little of that wonderful world that is the real world of catkind. That is a necessary, not just a pleasing, context. Fortunately, there is a lot of history behind the cat we know and love so much, and some stunning family ties. Best to seek them out. They complete the whole cloth from which our cat was cut.

Our companion cat almost certainly is descended from the North African wildcat, not to be confused with our own domestic cats that due to misadventure or our mismanagement return to the wild. Although we often hear them called wild, they are more properly called feral. The four-thousand-year-old domestication process for the cat is nothing when compared with the history of goats and dogs. Our modern domestic cats belong to a different species from their direct ancestors, but strangely enough they can still breed with the truly wild ones and on occasion, at least, do. They can also breed with the European wildcat, a particularly nasty bit of work that seems to be permanently angry with everything. Our house cats can even breed with the North American bobcat. In fact, there are any number of small cats around the world that can join with our pets and produce hybrids. Although the biology texts assure us that such matings should produce mules, that is, infertile offspring, that is not inevitably the case. There are some strange-looking cats running around the woods and it seems very likely that at least some wildcat blood has worked its way into the domestic cat line in places other than that aboriginal mix in North Africa. In all likelihood it happened in the primeval forests of Europe. All of that will probably not be proven in our time, but eventually work will be done with serum analysis and other advanced technologies and we will know a great deal more about all ancient affinities, our own included, than we do now.

And what are the cat's wild kin really like? People who first see wildcats (best done, by the way, in the wild), besides being excited almost beyond containment, comment on how catlike they are. That is an innocent case of careless semantics, of course. They should be catlike since they are in every sense cats, family *Felidae* in the Order Carnivora. But are these other cats, big as some of them are, really like our home-grown cat? A Siberian or Amur tiger can, after all, weigh between seven hundred and fifty and eight hundred pounds—outweighing a Siamese cat as much as two hundred to one.

Yes, cats are very much alike in more ways than we can possibly count. The cats of the world are amazingly and pleasingly consistent. Having been fortunate enough to have seen many hundreds of cats in the wild, I find the comparison inevitable and quite unavoidable. The cats I have watched the most (most often, for the longest time, and in the largest numbers) are lions, since I have spent time in Africa during each of the preceding nineteen years. An amalgamation of prides or loose feeding associations during the Serengeti migration can find anywhere from twenty to forty lions within a few hundred feet of each other living in temporary peace. Gluttony is a great equaliser. One thing about lions, with their huge yellow-gold eyes, they watch you with just as much

interest as you watch them, at least for short periods of time. In fact, that is about the most common experience people have with lions—reciprocal watching. I have read that lions cannot distinguish people as people when they approach in a vehicle because of carbon fumes, sound, shape or size, or some combination of factors. I am not sure that is true any more than I know what lions are thinking about when they do fix us with that penetrating cat stare of theirs. Are we lip-licking good as potential meals (very, very few lions are man-eaters, which I find strange), are we potential threats, or are we just a kind of animated cartoon and fun that way? When the cats in our house line up at the window and go cross-eyed staring at the bird feeder only inches away, we refer to it as cat television. We could very well be the sparrows in the lion's view of the world. It really is not possible to know about lions and their perception of us. Perhaps some day, if we allow lions to survive, we will be able to random-wire computers complex enough to simulate animal brains and type in the question, "What do you think, Simba: lunch, toy, or just a passing curiosity?"

In most areas where people encounter lions the great cats (up to about five hundred pounds) do not fear man. You can come to within a few feet of them as long as you are in a vehicle, and there the two of you can sit and watch each other. It is an interesting switch on the zoo experience: men, women, and children are on the inside looking out and the cats are looking in and free to do what they want. Inevitably the lions will become bored with you, yawn ever so impressively, and flop over onto their sides to sleep. When they aren't hunting they have a relatively short attention span. They will always know you are there, however.

On foot, one wants more distance, longer lenses, and a good pair of binoculars. Although few lions eat people, killing them is apparently a great outlet for machismo, or perhaps just fun. After all, we have killed tens of thousands of them for just those reasons. Fair is fair. In areas where there is still hunting in Africa (fortunately there are fewer such areas all the time), the cats don't watch you out in the open. Your view of a lion is usually of a tawny rear end vanishing into the nearest available undergrowth. You can be sure, however, that somewhere, out of sight, the cats are watching. You are never in wildcat country without being watched. That by definition.

Years ago I undertook a long-delayed task and began work on a book about the mountain lion or cougar or painter or panther, as it is known in Florida. Following my lifelong rule of trying never to write about animals and places that I have not observed first hand (I started my book about the African lion, *Mara Simba*, only after my fourteenth safari and finished it after my sixteenth), I went to the Everglades and began my search for one of the world's rarest and most elusive cats. I had observed the Florida race (I doubt that it is a subspecies) in captivity often and knew its habitat from experience, but I did want at least to see the cat in that habitat acting out a fragment of its natural life. An animal in its place adds a texture to your knowledge of it that can be gained in no other way. My quest was simply not to be successful.

The Florida panther saw me, however. Lots of times. Of that there can be no doubt. Time and again we would find brand-new spoor in the form of scats, or tracks or pug marks, but the cat always managed to get out of sight just in time. At one point we pointed our airboat, unfortunately a terribly noisy contraption, in towards a hammock or small Everglade island where a cat was thought to be. We jumped off into the muck and waded ashore. In the soft mud of the hammock beach were fresh tracks. They were so fresh the ridges between the pad marks were still stiff and firm. The marks had no water in them although firmly impressed in a matrix of very wet mud. As we squatted down to examine the evidence, the ridges in the tracks began to crumble and water seeped into the impressions, filling them up, absorbing them back into the island. They were soon history. It all took considerably less than two minutes and then they were no more. They were as irretrievably lost as just a moment ago.

There was no doubt we had missed seeing our ghostlike panther by fifteen seconds, hardly more than that. It had been watching us and almost certainly still was. With a good resident population of water moccasins and eastern diamondback rattlesnakes guaranteed nearby, it didn't seem wise to jump blindly over fallen logs and begin beating our way back into the thick tangle of undergrowth where we knew our panther had gone. The cat would just have moved ahead of us anyway, stopping to look and listen as we flopped and floundered about unable to see the ground beneath our feet. He would have moved in circles for as long as we chose to play his game, rather than moving off the hammock into the open water where he would lose control of when he was being seen. He was calling the shots on his own home ground. Cats like that position of command. It suits them perfectly. They watch you when they want to. You watch them . . . when they want you to. It is the very essence of being a cat.

Leopards are much the same way. In the nearly twenty years that my wife and I have been leading photographic safaris in Africa, we always have given the same initial advice to people who announce that they are particularly interested in cats—and that is a very high percentage of the people who choose to go to Africa.

"We will get you all the lion you can possibly want. We will see cheetah although the number is unpredictable. You can see ten in a day or one in a week in the same general area. As for leopard, they will see us. If they so elect, we will see them."

It always works out just that way. The wildcats have excellent hearing, incredible eyesight, and a good enough sense of smell to let them track any intruder minute by minute after he crosses over into the cat's territory or block. They know their home ground intimately. They have to. It feeds them and protects them and they are linked to it as we could never be. They always have you well monitored, and in non-hunting areas or blocks they may very well expose themselves to scrutiny, but only if and when they are in the mood.

Black panthers or black leopards (they are exactly the same animal) represent nothing more than a colour phase of the spotted leopard. The leopard in Asia and Africa (the common leopard, specifically, not the snow or clouded leopards) is also the same animal. The species has, then, an enormous geographic range as well as that range in colour.

A black or nearly black coat can be a severe handicap for a cat that hunts on generally flat land in golden sunlit grasses. For that reason the black phase is relatively rare in East Africa, in most of Africa for that matter, and fairly common in the jungles of the Malay Peninsula and in parts of India. Spotted leopards and black panthers can be littermates and one can give birth to the other. It is just that the gene for that melanistic variation is stronger in the more appropriate settings, areas of dark shadows where sun stippling is not emulated with any profit.

The way that works is simple enough. Cub mortality among wildcats is high, as high as 50 per cent. So the animals are constantly selecting for the best combination of attributes. Leopards that are black and carry the black phase gene tend to survive better and thus reproduce more often in

Black panther

areas where it is useful to be black. They would also find it easier to hunt and feed their cubs, so that more cubs carrying that gene would survive in the proper setting. But there are certainly areas where hunting success is made lower by the dark colour. Camouflage is not a nicety for predators, it is just about a necessity. Prey animals are alert or their species would be extinct. I had seen a great many leopard in both Africa and Asia, always spotted leopard, and really didn't expect ever to see a black leopard outside a captive cat population. Not many people do, and although I have spent much of my life looking at wildlife when I wasn't enjoying our collection of domestic animals at home, seeing a glimpse of the black leopard just didn't seem all that realistic, although like everyone else I have my "hope" or "wish" list. Luck, fortunately, had plans for me that I knew nothing about.

In the first instance we were driving from Colombo, the capital of Sri Lanka, to the great Buddhist shrine known as Sigiriya. There are huge boulders in the area (Sigiriya itself is a single rock that used to have a city built on top of it). As we passed a mere pebble of a boulder, about the size of a two-storey house, I thought I saw something very, very black perched on top of it. It was a fleeting sight, literally out of the corner of my eye. I didn't even have a chance to turn my head. My first impression was that it was a goat, for goats are often jet black and they scramble all over the rocks in the area, acrobats and clowns that they are. As we moved away, though, I began seeing an instant replay and became more and more certain that I hadn't seen a goat at all, but something quite different, something quite wonderful. I apologised to my travelling companion, the ever good-natured science-fiction genius Arthur C. Clarke, and asked the driver to turn round. As we rounded the boulder, my glasses came up and there in perfect ten-power magnification was an honest-to-goodness black leopard. The beast could be added to my top-priority list and be checked off at the same time. The leopard looked directly into the lenses of my binoculars and fixed me with the steadiest stare I have ever seen in anything but a bird of prey or a snake. The tip of his tail was twitching expressively but his stare was anything but twitchy. I was riveted in place, nailed down by two yellow eyes that would not let me loose. He had me fixed as surely as if he had held me in his claws. Then in true cat fashion the big one (135 to 150 pounds, I would estimate) flopped over and slept. I had given him all the amusement I had to offer. I was boring him, and that is something no cat big or small will ever tolerate. And, indeed, why should they? They can always retreat to what is undoubtedly a very rich internal life.

When we got back to Colombo I had some tepid tea with the head of the Wildlife Department. It is not only possible but easy to get a bad reputation by reporting unlikely wildlife sightings, so I played it as cool as I could. It happened to be particularly important with Mr. da Sylva because his moods were often cranky and his attitudes were more difficult to predict than that of any of the leopards in his charge. In fact, he didn't like Americans or Europeans and was seldom reluctant to let you know.

"How often do you see black leopards?" I asked in seeming innocence.

"From time to time," came his rather bored answer, "but there is one moving around in the rocks near Sigiriya now. We have had several reports this month on him. A big male, apparently."

Then I blurted it out. I had in fact watched the black leopard of Sigiriya watching me.

Three hundred and sixty-four days later I was moving at about thirty-five miles an hour down a long and dusty dirt road in the Maasai Mara area of southern Kenya with Aslam, our driver of many years. It was just after ten o'clock in the morning and the sun was high and very bright. The Mara is barely south of the Equator, less than one degree south. It is actually the Serengeti uplands, a broad savannah with only scattered trees isolated on hillsides and down along riverbanks. (The technical definition of a savannah is open country where the mean distance between the trunks of the trees is greater than the area enclosed beneath the canopy.) The widely dispersed clumps of trees in the Mara are used by leopard, spotted leopard, and the vast open expanses by an enormous number of lion and a respectable population of cheetah. Three other cats, the caracal, serval, and African wildcat, also hunt the area but for much smaller prey. The number of hoofed animals that may be moving through the area at one time can number close to two million since the Maasai Mara is the northern terminus of the great looping Serengeti migration. It is an open ground hunter's paradise.

As we were moving along the road, we could see virtually no vegetation heavier than grasses and sedges on either side of the road for miles, and even they had been chomped down to a stubble by the vast herds grazing nearby. The nearest trees were miles away up on the slopes of the Great Rift Valley. Suddenly, from our right, something very long and slab-sided with an enormously long tail, something very black, back-lit as it was, came bounding across the open area towards the road. It sprinted across a thousand feet of the stubble grass, shot across the road, and covered another thousand feet of open space to our left before disappearing into a depression. By the time the animal hit the road and crossed it in two strides we were nearly on top of him. We saw him at a distance of about a dozen feet. There was simply no possibility that we were mistaken. We both gaped. Aslam stopped the van and we sat looking at each other. At the same time we reached out and shook hands and then Aslam drove on. He shook his head from time to time, and so did I. That cat just didn't belong there, not in the Mara, not in daylight, not in a treeless area, not in the open.

Again, the professional observer simply has to protect his reputation at all costs. Too many amateurs see far too many things that are simply not there. This is due generally to wishful thinking more than the conscious intent to be dishonest. Still, it is inaccurate and generally not forgiven. I said nothing about the black leopard in the Mara when I got back to Nairobi until a few days later over dinner when a member of the Kenya Wildlife Department volunteered the advice that I should be sure to keep my eyes open when I was next down in that area. There was a black leopard being reported by the game rangers there. It could be a half century or more before another appeared.

Seeing two black leopards so near to each other in time if not in geography was a great thrill. Seeing one on an open African savannah was really exciting because it was so unlikely a thing to happen. But there was one great difference. The cat in Sri Lanka was watching me, and somehow that was the way things should have been. Everything was in its place: species, time and perspective. He was relaxed, he was high up, he was almost hidden from view, although that didn't seem to be very important to him, and he was watching the world variously creep and dash by below him, most of it not even aware that he was there overseeing it all. How perfectly catlike! He could watch when he felt he needed distraction, or he could sleep. He belonged to the largest truly terrestrial predator species

Lynx

on the island, and with the exception of a rare chance encounter with a particularly large and aggressive python, he had nothing to fear. Pythons aren't rare, not in Sri Lanka, but ones that elect to tangle with large leopards are. Mugger crocodiles in Sri Lanka's waterholes or tanks could take an occasional leopard, one supposes, but it wasn't something our leopard appeared to be thinking about when we encountered him.

In contrast, our black leopard in the Maasai Mara, although thrilling to see, somehow lacked the same dignity. We had taken something from him by even seeing him, although that had hardly been our intent. We caught a cat that was to some degree disadvantaged in life by his dark colouration out in the open. He clearly did not want to be observed and was sprinting for all he was worth to get out of sight on a very hot day in very bright light. That was not the way it was supposed to be with that species. An enormously powerful leopard of any colour should be spared the indignity of flight. Watching can be a mark of superiority, while being watched suggests a kind of helplessness when you can't watch back on terms you choose. In the predator and prey relationship, that is often literally true.

And so it is with the other wildcat species. And in all of this there is a clue for people who are addicted to nature on television. Many of them, perhaps most when they are all accounted for, fake it. That is not necessarily a bad thing because it still allows the public to see the right animals in the right places with a conservation message that is inevitably on the side of the angels. It is just that the animals used as models, especially cats, are not truly wild-living animals but captives that have been socialised. Example: a half-hour tape about the "home life" of a cougar and her cubs. We see her nursing her young, hunting prey, bringing back a haunch of something to start her offspring on solid food. If not with the first, then certainly with the second change of camera angle, you should be reasonably certain you are seeing pictorial licence at work. The cat is a captive and very used to people controlling it. No camera person was ever slick enough to move around in a cat's territory secretly and watch her being intimate with anything. The cat knows the camera and its operator are there long before the camera person knows a cat is there for the focusing. It is all very simple. In the wild as much as or perhaps even more than in our homes, except in very rare circumstances, a cat is watching.

17

Last week our son, Clay, his wife, Sheila (with child), and our first grandson, Joshua, came back from Guam. It had been a long two years but the young doctor and his expanding family were home. One of the many reunions and events, perhaps a small one in comparison with the others, was the reunion of Clay with his two surviving cats, Xnard and Squid. There is a long rabies quarantine period on Guam, so his cats had stayed with us rather than being put through all that stress. (Mr. Bill, a tom they adopted on Guam, disappeared one day and was never seen again. They looked everywhere for him as they knew their time there was winding down but without any luck. If he is alive, Mr. Bill is undoubtedly still hunting little lizards on the warm rocks of a sunny Pacific island.)

But something extra and unpleasant had happened here. Two days before the Guam contingent was due, Jill was driving out of our driveway and Xnard shot out from under a bush. We did not know how badly he was hurt, if he was really hurt at all, because after the car passed over him he vanished into a marsh not far from the house. We looked for him but could not find a single clue as to where he had gone in the frozen tangle. We didn't even know if he was alive. Jill was not looking forward to greeting her son with the news that she had run over his cat.

That night Xnard came home and mewed pitifully to come in. He had patches of fur missing, dried blood showed where he had bitten the inside of his mouth, but he didn't react badly to manipulation and he was subjected to it from end to end. Apparently no wheel had passed over him; still, he had somehow been pretty well roughed up. He would certainly live although he would be very stiff for a while. By morning he was eating jars of soft baby food which are kept on hand for emergencies. In another twenty-four hours his favourite person in the world would be home. It wasn't going to be so bad after all.

We explained the situation to Clay on the way to the farm from the airport and he decided to let Xnard take the lead. We came in and Xnard's head came up from his resting roost. He looked at Clay and obviously listened to his voice. His eyes followed Clay wherever he went in the room. We left the room to show the rest of the new house to Clay and Sheila and then came back again. Xnard looked at Clay intently and Clay realised what he was supposed to do. He sat down and then Xnard arose, still stiff but able to negotiate the move, jumped down, and came over to the chair. Before he could jump to Clay's lap, which was obviously going to be painful for him, Clay picked him up as if he were a Fabergé egg. Xnard settled down, half closed his eyes, and began to purr. Everything was back in place.

Two years is a human concept based on some rather refined astronomical measurements and it seems clear enough that a cat couldn't grasp any of it, not as a precise calculation. But *long time*, as we have indicated elsewhere, could be a reality. For Xnard, what had it been, and could he have anticipated it would come to an end? Other owners and other places had vanished from his life never to reappear. Because Clay was part of a benevolent experience (except the part about the Subaru), would or indeed could Xnard have anticipated his world remaining intact despite the gaps?

Time is perhaps our prime yardstick. The distance to a friend's home is generally calculated by how long it takes to get there rather than by the number of actual miles it is, for time is the reality given varying road, traffic, and weather conditions, and alternate routes, and distance isn't, not really. Because we have office hours, make dates, keep appointments, catch trains, planes, and buses, listen to the radio and watch television, time is essential to us. Things stay in the oven for precise lengths of time, babies take nine months, we can beat traffic if we get away by three—we surround ourselves with realities that depend on one other dominant reality, the inexorable passage of time, a precisely measurable phenomenon.

We have discussed how cats can take seasonal clues and other elapsed time measurements not as time but as triggers and alarms when there are things they have to do. But when Xnard closed his eyes, did he know it had been a long time, and what did he feel because of it? As far as I can tell, and judging from the conversations I have had with other people who know animal behaviour, those are questions we are not likely ever to be able to answer, although *ever* remains a very troublesome word for me. Unless, though, there is some incredible breakthrough that allows us to discuss abstract matters with animals as bright as cats and dogs (and that just doesn't seem likely at the moment), how could we ever know?

The smarter and more sophisticated we get, the brighter animals appear to be. That is natural enough. The smarter a person or society gets, the less the individual people need to have dumb things around them to lord it over and feel superior to. That works with the relationship between different kinds of humans just as it works between humans and animals. We have come to a time when we can emotionally tolerate animals being cognitive so, by decree as well as by degree, they are. What are some of the things that happened to Xnard during that somewhat traumatic but in the end joyful forty-eight hours?

He was in a new home, on a farm, not all that familiar with the ins and outs. Allow him that. But there was a driveway precisely ninety-six feet long that led to his last place of residence. He knew both driveways (the new one being much the longer) and cars. Dashing under a car was careless or not very bright or a bit of both. He ran away, immediately, and hid. That was instinctive and generally the right thing to do. Harm was afoot, and until it could be fully comprehended and evaluated, it was best to get out of its way. Interestingly enough, any number of vets have told me that dogs hit by cars are most often injured in the rear, cats most often in the head and the front of their bodies. Apparently, if that is true, cats turn and face their attacker at the last minute if flight is not working. Still, given the opportunity, a cat will get under cover at a safe distance when things start harming and hurting.

Xnard stayed hidden for hours and then made a decision, however cats arrive at such determinations, to go home. It must have hurt to walk and he must have felt vulnerable, but he did the sensible thing. He came home where he would have remembered it would be warmer, where there would be water to drink, and where it would be dry. He probably wasn't very hungry that first night. For cats appetite is the first thing to go when they don't feel well. That move out of hiding was just plain sensible, with undoubtedly some instinctive overlay having to do with dens and safety.

Then there was the twenty-four-hour resting period when he allowed people he knows and likes to handle him. Did he know it was for his own

good? I doubt it, not intellectually; kittens let their mothers examine them so it could be instinctive. But he did trust us. That was from his experience with us. That was sensible.

When he ate the next day it was probably instinct and an inside signal. Does that signal shut off when a cat is seriously ill and might be better off without loading up for a short period of time? We can't tell, not really. If it is an instinctive shutdown, it can quickly become a seriously misplaced one, for cats off their feed get weaker and certainly become dehydrated. They sometimes have to be tube-fed to keep them alive. It is difficult to say how that would work in a case like Xnard's, but he did eat, however slowly and carefully. He was hurting, but jars of baby food are very tempting and easy to manage.

Then the precious signal, Clay's voice. Xnard probably heard Clay before he saw him, and in fact we don't know which signal, the way Clay looks or the way he sounds, would be more significant. By some means, or more likely a combination of means, Xnard found out that something important had come back into his life. As bedraggled as he was from the vicious Subaru attack, he watched Clay with apparent intensity and then, when Clay was in a manageable position, Xnard for all his aching bones and sore muscles made the move to reconnect.

What Xnard feels for Clay is not really possible for us to define. He almost never stops looking at him if he is in the room, and as the days have progressed Xnard is making more certain that he follows Clay and gets into a position to watch him (they did, after all, go through medical school and a fearful internship together). Is it love? The word is far too loaded, far too anthropocentric. We need another way to express the way animals feel about us, at least on the positive side. The negatives, some of them, work. Animals fear some people: fear is a negative emotional experience (as well as a practical consideration) but it isn't reaching when we use it. Animals don't like some people? Yes, that is true, they show it all the time and are never diplomatic about it. But what about *hate*? Dare we say that an animal *hates* someone? We say it all the time, but hate, like love, carries an awful lot of emotional baggage with it and probably is not the best use of language. As a matter of fact, in people, hate is at least as intense an emotion as love. Of course, swinging the other way for a moment, we are pretty loose with such words. We hate a movie yet love a flavour of ice cream. Kids hate liver and spinach but love a coach or a new

Michael Jackson record. If we are that loose with the love and hate of the inanimate things and distant almost mythic people in our lives, why can't we let animals hate and love? Because when you are seriously trying to establish a context for understanding anything as bewildering as a cat, it is better to avoid at least the obvious pitfalls of obfuscating language and mangled comprehension.

But Xnard watched Clay, remembered Clay, thought about Clay in the way cats do that, and despite his own freshly inflicted trauma reacted to Clay appropriately. It is the way cats seem to expect things to happen. They wait and they watch and things come full circle. The minor glitches pass (if they don't kill you first) and the important things happen in their own good time. That is probably why it pays for cats to sleep so much. It makes the waiting time pass more quickly for them.

18

We have an enormous amount of traditional information about cats, and misinformation as well, of course. It is not at all clear which list is longer. I suspect the latter. But it all adds up to lore. Cats have been sculpted, painted, moulded, drawn, charcoaled, etched, mummified, deified, televised, and photographed. There are poems, odes, short stories, long stories, and novels about cats. There are essays, technical papers, and scientific volumes, too. A friend of mine assembled over four thousand books on cats before he died, and he still had a long way to go. When you add oral tradition, religion, nonsense, and the inevitable spooky stuff to all of this, plus ephemera like postcards, product logos, and greeting cards, the sheer bulk is overwhelming. Dolls, stuffed toys, games, ditties, and songs; it never seems to stop. But all of that is our knowledge, fine and faulty both, of the cat, gained because we have watched cats intently for four millennia. We do that mostly in our homes today, but before that we saw them as wild creatures to admire as objects of beauty, to fear as hunters, and to destroy so that we could get their fur (which is just about the poorest fur there is when it comes to practical considerations like keeping warm).

We have also hunted cats because, although I have somehow failed to pick up on this, it is fun to kill them. (Quite frankly, I have always felt that anyone who could derive pleasure from killing a lion, leopard, tiger, puma, jaguar, or any other cat for that matter, was an incipient sociopath and should be held suspect. I feel the same way about ladies who wear them. They have to be watched carefully.)

Since cats watch us, what forms do their observations, impressions, and reactions take? Cats are not creators of things as we are and do not appear to have any oral traditions that we can interpret, so their view of us is much more immediate, of much shorter duration. It goes with their being existential hedonists. In fact, the human "lore" cats have available to work with is probably limited to two generalised forms, if that. There is the conditioning of the individual, and *possibly* something that somehow has worked its way into the cat's genetic package and has literally become part of the animal, part of its instincts. It would have had to happen in near-record time. More on that in a moment.

Conditioning is easy to accomplish, and although its mechanisms can be as obscure in any individual cat as the history of that single animal is obscure, the results can be read. A kitten cuddled from birth will be a cuddler all its life, if not unexpectedly and seriously traumatised by people. Even then, a former person-loving cat can be tolerant beyond belief and give the human species another chance again and again. That may be due to the relative intensities of the experiences or to actual differences between cats. It is difficult to quantify, hard even to interpret. We don't know how the inherent differences between animals manifest themselves and how far conditioning ameliorates or intensifies them.

Our recently inherited barn cats (one of which has already been to the vet to be spayed, wormed, and given its shots, including feline leukemia and rabies) may or may not have been traumatised before we inherited them, but they certainly were on the wild side when we got here. They were not the products of early-on cuddling, clearly. But just by feeding them we seem to have broken through, and we can touch two out of the three without trouble. Number three is showing signs of coming round. One day the Thistle Hill Regulars will sit on our laps and together we will laugh about the early spooky days when we were so untrustworthy and they so untrusting. At first I didn't think that day would come but now I am certain it will. The gap is closing.

But deeper, way inside their very being, what human lore do cats carry? It is my impression that there is very little there, if anything at all. There appears to be evidence to support this view. The wariness cats sometimes exhibit around people seems to be no different from the way they react to strange cats, dogs, horses, cardboard boxes, or anything else that suddenly enters their essentially neat little worlds. General wariness or caution is instinctive, but I doubt that that has anything to do with the number of legs we have. I don't think we caused any of it or inspired it.

Cats that are born as feral animals show a great interest in people, as we

have discussed. Barn cats watch people as carefully as our pillow weights do. And when it is cold and wet, they come to our shelters and they accept food. If any of that is instinct beyond the natural tendency to be opportunistic, it is in their positive column. I suspect it is nothing more than opportunism, however. I think they would take advantage of what chimpanzees or gorillas had to offer if their observations had convinced them that the apes were benign. And so for that matter would we.

When Xnard got Subarued in our driveway, he came home within a matter of hours. Whatever his instincts may have been to flee the scene of a trauma, he still worked his way back not so much to a place, because the place is new to him, but to people he trusted and perhaps felt in some way that he needed. All of that had to be the result of conditioning. It is obvious that we make him feel good when he is around us, and that cold night with all of his bruises he wanted above all, I am sure, to feel good, or at least better.

In fact, as I watch cats, and I certainly do that, I see all kinds of instincts flood to the fore triggered by everything from a bird at the feeder to loud and sudden noises that could announce trouble (and perhaps hurt), to new animals that have to be evaluated, to warm places near heaters, to soft things like pillows. I see a natural drift towards any form of hedonism and, as a grandfather, I see the acceptance of almost any amount of handling by some cats and very low tolerance for mauling in others. But I detect nothing that I can really ascribe to instinctive behaviour towards human beings as a species. We are creatures ourselves in the grand view of the big scheme, and cats react to all creatures with some instinctive elements. None of it, as far as I can detect, is specific to our kind.

It is easy enough to understand that, too. We have had a singularly short interactive history with them as domestic animals. I don't know how long it takes to get information worked down into a gene somewhere, and I don't know anybody with that information (or I would ask them), but it must be longer than four thousand years. We really didn't need a domestic cat until the Egyptians invented the silo and began storing their crops. When the mice found out, they put out the word and engaged in one long picnic. The better mousetrap had to be adapted from wild stock. That was barely two thousand years before the dawn of Christianity. When we speak of wild species and their behavioural evolution, we speak of hundreds of thousands of years and sometimes millions. (Example:

dogs and bears had a common ancestor in Miacis, *sixty million years ago.*) It just doesn't seem likely that we have been the cause of much in the way of instinctive changes or additions in the short time there has been anything like domestic cats. They probably had all the instincts they needed from the outset to handle us—peculiar as we may be.

There is another factor: the matter of training. Dogs have been with us for possibly as long as twenty to twenty-five thousand years. That is five to six times as long as the cat. (And in some places goats *may* have come even before the dog.) Dogs have been trained as cats really never have been. Some people have taught individual cats to do tricks, but cats in general have always had as their chief assignment our aesthetic satisfaction. The cat's one economic value has been a result of an instinct, hunting small animals like mice and rats. Cats not only take obvious pleasure in pouncing on their prey, they sometimes eat what they catch. That has given them some real value, but it is piddling. The fact that some people eat cats is of little real economic significance and perfectly awful as an aesthetic consideration.

Dogs are different. Anyone who has ever seen a border collie work sheep or a mastiff derivative protect his owner's property or a Komondor fend off bears and wolves or a Saluki run down game or a northern spitz derivative pull sleds, has to see that dogs have not only been designed by breeding to handy physical sizes and styles but otherwise equipped to serve in special ways. I suspect their specialised behaviour has become instinct rather quickly as these things would seem to go. Even twenty-five centuries isn't all that long a time, but border collies are so intent on herding that as puppies you had better give them work to do or they will herd the piano, the sofa, and your elderly Aunt Minnie as an outlet for what has been built into them. And retrievers have to retrieve, as anyone with experience with a golden or a Labrador can tell you. It doesn't take very much encouragement to get a Doberman to be territorial or for a terrier to bark at a knock on the door. That pretty much has to be all instinct by now.

But is that it for the cat? No, there is a subheading under conditioning. Empirical conditioning can be passed along. Kittens, we know, are not precocious. The time spent with their mother (and very often no other cat but the mother, since most queens will shred any living thing, particularly a cat, that comes too near their precious brood) is learning time. If the

mother jumps at the sight or sound of a dog because of an earlier experience in her life, her kittens will almost surely pick up on the tension and be dog haters and fearers all their lives, too. That may come down through multiple generations. Maybe a cat hates dogs if its great-grandmother hated dogs and there has been no intervening experience by a predecessor to offset that reaction. Enough generations may an instinct make if it contributes in the very long run to survivability and breedability. It can be overcome with intensive and painstaking reconditioning in any one generation, but it isn't easy and may prove to be a failing enterprise after a lot of patient work. Feral queens that fear people will have very wild kittens that are generally all but unredeemable.

The queen among our Thistle Hill Regulars was not really a people hater, obviously. She was naturally wary of strangers and perhaps of people in general, but not hysterical. She did have and still has, in fact, a profound sense of the dramatic and likes to duck and peek and duck again, but she isn't really a hater. Her kittens, then, aren't either. They have picked up the caution behaviour (reinforced no doubt by their own instincts about all things that belong to the unknown), but that is neither hate nor terror. How much is a game is hard to determine.

So, if I am right, cats have an instinctive knowledge of mankind taken directly from their instinctive knowledge of all other life forms but probably little if to any degree modified by anything that is peculiarly us. They are conditioned by us from birth, however, and they do show variations by breed and by individual personalities, if we may borrow that word despite the fact that it contains a specific reference to "person". They also show evidence of conditioning by parental reactions, but that is peculiar to all mammals where there is parental care. The fact that most intelligent animals tend to spend long learning periods suggests that conditioning by parental example is almost always terribly important to the higher intellectual estate. All the mammals identified as Carnivora spend long periods with one or more parents. So do the primates and the whales. Guinea pigs and jackrabbits are off almost immediately after birth. Why not? What can a guinea pig or hare teach anyone?

19

The fact that we destroy somewhere between 13 and 15 million dogs and cats (including a very high percentage of puppies and kittens) each year for the want of proper homes is a nightmare that we should never have learned to live with, but we have. All it takes to avoid that ongoing calamity is spaying and neutering, but we just aren't doing it. We have not reached that level of compassion or responsibility. One has to believe that it will come in time. To accept that it won't would be, well, unthinkable. What is going to happen in less advantaged societies boggles the mind. It may be millennia yet before cats in India and Burma and most of Africa get any consideration at all except from a handful of people.

Clearly, for all their intelligence, neither dogs nor cats can understand any of these terrible concerns. The only other dogs and cats in the world that exist for them are those they encounter, even if that is done only by smell, pheromones on a hydrant or hubcap, a scrape in some soil or sand. None of our companion animals could grasp concepts involving statistics, large numbers, unseen and otherwise undetected animals, ovariohysterectomies or castration. They don't even understand, we are sure, any relationship between a sexual encounter and pregnancy and birth, and therefore could not understand the necessity or techniques for interfering with the process. They seem closed off from their own mortality and the peril of it all. That level of comprehension would appear to be ours alone. But is it?

We approach such matters with the intellect of unconcern, largely, although we have started to beget the odd humanitarian in our species and that bodes well for the future. The mutation that produces compassion might take hold, if that is how things are done in evolution. Is our angle of attack the only one? Animals—I have heard it said and seen it written scores of times—have no comprehension of their own mortality. They can't understand death, this line of logic takes us, because they can't understand life. An animal battling to save its life or escape peril is being driven by that mighty force called instinct and doesn't think of the situation as it really is. They say our animals do not fear death but just fear what is going on, like being bitten, chased, gored, stepped on, or scratched. Maybe—and maybe not.

Studies of cats by Antoine Watteau

In her nearly three decades along the shore of Lake Tanganyika in Tanzania, at her Gombe Research Station, Dr. Jane Goodall has watched chimpanzees in just about every situation available to the species as a life experience. She has seen chimpanzee mothers with stillborn young or with a baby that due to postnatal mischance or birth defects didn't survive. These females were clearly in mourning. All the local chimps seemed in fine fettle when I was there, but Dr. Goodall showed me photographs. A chimpanzee in deep depression is as easily recognised as a human being in the same condition. I have personally seen baboons with babies so long dead they had begun to disintegrate still carrying or dragging the bodies around, and I have seen other members of the troop come to look at a dead infant and cluck over it. I have seen primates try to get dead infants to nurse. It simply is not possible to conclude that these animals were unaware of death when they were in its presence. They just had to learn they could not fix it. But thinking about it before it happens is something else, and I don't think anyone can know a great deal about how much of that animals do. Death, though, is a reality to at least the more intelligent animals. It certainly is to elephants, who carry on and mourn in what appears to be a ritualistic fashion.

Ah, but chimpanzees and baboons are primates and elephants have an intelligence range clearly far above that of the Carnivora. What of cats and dogs? One factor: chimpanzees, baboons, and elephants don't have litters. A cat with seven kittens or a dog with five to fifteen puppies has lots of other things to occupy her attention. Nature could only allow them an absolute minimum of mourning time for that is essentially downtime and the other young, those that still matter to the species, would suffer if the mother were to concentrate on one or even two dead babies. As nature is always worried about species rather than individuals, the female cat, in our discussion here, would only be allowed to carry the dead baby away. The reasons for the removal are probably two-fold. The smell of the dead baby, quickly to become carrion, would attract troublesome animals that could endanger the litter's surviving members; and there is the matter of disease. Not the least of the troublesome animals would be insects, of course. No dog or cat wants her nest full of buzzing flies and burrowing maggots.

I have seen female cats who have been too old or too young to breed bear a single offspring and then have it die. It does depress them and they do go around looking for it after it has been taken away by owners. I have seen a Labrador bitch try to get a dead puppy to nurse just as the monkey did.

I once had to interview the wife of a law enforcement officer who had been killed in the line of duty. I will never forget her words:

"I wanted so much for that not to be. I thought if I just go outside and rake leaves, act normally, it will go away."

Obviously I am not suggesting anything remotely like a comparison, but that is just the way I have seen both dogs and cats act when they did not have the imperative of surviving littermates to demand their attention. They tried to pretend it wasn't so by doing their instinctive things they were organised to do, even after their noses told them to forget it.

All of this leads me to believe that at some level cats do have some primitive sense ("primitive" means simply that it is too complex for us to understand) of mortality, some relationship to the end of life. They may not deal with their own mortality, we can't prove that they do, at least, but they do seem to get the gist of it when it is someone or something they "love". (We still haven't become comfortable with animals loving and hating, you will recall.) Death close to home does depress them, though, and I just don't know if it is possible for an animal to be depressed (emotionally without apparent physical cause) without some level of awareness of the basic problem.

There is a seemingly endless supply of apocryphal stories about pets going into deep decline over the death of their human companions. In Scotland, Greyfriar's Bobby would not leave his master's grave for fourteen years and died there, protecting it. Friends of the old man brought the dog food and water every day through all those years. It is a heck of a yarn and is good for tourism if it isn't literally true, but they swear in Edinburgh it is fact. The story gets to me. I even bought a sculpture of the little dog.

For years cats have wailed at midnight or at the exact moment of their master or mistress's death. Ghost cats have left paw prints in the snow or mud going to and from a loved one's grave, even though the animal was never seen. Stories like these go on forever and they are like psi-trailing. You are welcome to treat them as you wish. It is the listener or reader who is served by such stories, reinforced in some way, and they are there for the having. Taking them apart or vigorously denying them is about as sensible—and as necessary—as attacking someone's religion or their very personal relationship with their own destiny. People who want to believe in Heaven and Hell—and in Greyfriar's Bobby and psi-trailing cats— should be completely free to do so without our pounding on their intellects demanding to be heard.

There is a seductive tendency to assume that cats are where they are in their evolutionary stage of development through some form of pre-ordination. There is far too much chance in life for that to work. A change in weather patterns can bring new animals into an area where they have never been before and they could offer new patterns of threat either directly or as competition for food and shelter. That could cause the cat to change. Disease or competition could thin out the ranks or exterminate a species whose existence held the cat back and allow the cat to expand into new niches with new opportunities. If small rodents didn't live in some areas where they now flourish because there were too many snakes, for instance, the cat might be a snake hunter rather than a rat and mouse catcher, and that would require a different package of senses and reflexes. Snakes aren't much good at fleeing, but although they are very fragile creatures, they sure are good at fighting back. Constrictors and venomous species would make the cat a lot more careful than it is now about when, where, and how it hits its prey. A drop in ambient temperature might favour rodents and drive snakes away. Cats do take lizards, but what if more than just the two species of lizard—the Gila monster and Mexican beaded lizard—were venomous? What if many or even all of the world's lizards were? Cats would probably not hunt lizards, or would have different reflexes or a different body chemistry to enable them to tolerate intoxication—or some of all three.

It is true, obviously, that species that interact over a very long period of time affect each other's evolutionary course, but still there is so much chance involved that preordination just doesn't cut it. A cat has become a cat because of all the things that can happen to a cat in the course of its species' development. We became what we are for exactly the same reasons. Climate and climatic changes (like ice ages, for instance), seismic activity, geothermal activity, the evolution of or invasion by new species, the coming and going of food supplies, disease, perhaps mutations, solar phenomena (like a sudden increase in ultraviolet radiation that can cause

our immune systems to be seriously compromised), meteor impact, and perhaps, just perhaps, the appearance of a super intellect or two in succession that results in inventions that change the course of events (fire, stone chipping, any form of more advanced weaponry like the throwing stick, the use of skins—these may come on slowly or may be actually invented—we don't know), all of these things could change our course. Simpler events could change the cat's course.

By chance, we have come into prolonged contact with cats. We have had some input but not the whole or last word in their evolution as companion animals. They probably have changed us, too, but in ways it will take a very long time for us to work out. Since it seems evident now that people who bond to pets live longer and are generally more compassionate, it may very well be that people with pets produce more children and then undoubtedly influence those children in their own ways and affections. If that is so, then cats have been influencing the breeding of pet owners to remain pet owners and perhaps to intensify their interaction with their pets. And all the time we thought we were breeding cats to please us. It is just as likely that they have been "breeding" us to please them!

None of this was foreordained, however. We must enter it all into the book as one of the world's happiest set of accidents. One little change in the early history of either of our species could have sent us all off in very different directions and we wouldn't be watching cats with any great interest, nor they us.

20

Cat-watching people like nothing better, it seems, than talking about the people-watching cats they have known and loved. That has led us to try to explore some of the ways cats might perceive us or at least accommodate the invaluable information that we exist within their sphere of influence. To understand exactly how difficult a task that is for us, or perhaps to realise how impossible it actually is, at least for the time being, consider how we might describe to each other (fellow humans) what we see as individuals.

I can say and you can acknowledge that a cat in a typical display of hedonism lies curled on a large, soft cushion before us. It is sleeping. We can share in our conversation certain descriptions of the cat's shape, size, and texture, by feeling the cat, lifting the cat, smelling it, and listening to it exclaim when we disturb its sleep, or purr if it finds our handling to its liking. We can appear to agree on all points, but does each of us really know what the other is talking about? We can photograph the cat in place and see its photograph in under a minute. We can videotape it and have instant replay in colour, life-size if we have a large screen. We can have a friend draw or paint it, perhaps sculpt it, and thereby introduce yet another observer. We have many ways of reproducing its image. With modern medical imaging techniques we can see inside it, even slice by slice with a CAT scan (that may be one of the world's most profound, unintentional, in fact, unavoidable puns). We can tell our computers what we see and have that information digitalised and replayed as words or pictures or both. We can relay the information to a satellite in synchronous orbit above our planet and those data can be accessed in Russia or China, Kenya or Cairo. The ways and the means we have of storing, retrieving, and relaying the information that a sleeping cat lies before us are incredibly complex and seemingly without end. But can anyone possibly know what we are seeing that inspires our signals?

In the presence of the cat itself, we do have texture and odour as reinforcers (one supposes we could also taste the animal but that is not a very attractive idea). Once we step back and use any imaging technique we have at our disposal, however, we take a truly giant step away from the full reality of our subject cat. We can see the images and, to a somewhat less satisfactory degree for most of us, we can listen to recordings of everything from its heartbeat to its yowls, purrs, and hisses. But that is it. When not in the presence of the cat, we lose almost all of the reinforcement we are capable of absorbing. Even the emotional impact of reproduced images is dead when compared to the real thing. True artists have been fighting (rapidly) toward computer imaging as a real art form and not a gimmick.

The important point is that no matter how we have reproduced or imaged the cat (or anything else, of course), there is still a link that has to be made, and we can think of it as the ultimate link of uncertainty. We are each alone with our brains, and have to see or hear the cat as individuals. No one alive or dead can share what we each experience, not for sure, not for so much as one second. That is the uncertainty part. I can tell you what I see in an image, whichever one I choose, but my words cannot be anything but subjective. You can hear what I say, but that is at least as subjective. And there is an additional uncertainty factor here to widen the gulf. Included in your impression of the cat as *I* saw it will be your impression of me and any feelings you have or don't have about me. They will certainly colour the experience for you. It works the same way in reverse. You cannot hear with my ears and I cannot see with your eyes, and the cat remains that giant step removed from each of us, yet for each of us it is an experience unique and apart.

If we are not imaging the cat but seeing it together alive before us, it will be no different at all. We have our own sensory arrays and we will each struggle to get through to the other what we perceive to be the true cat of reality, or at least as it is so very real to each of us. The problem is, and apparently will remain for some time to come, that it *is* subjective, and incoming impressions on optic or auditory nerves cannot be swapped. The best we can do at this stage of our development is interpret, verbalise, and then interpret again. It doesn't matter a fig whether it is the cat or the image of a cat. And that, we can assume, is why they invented poetry. It is as good an explanation as any for imaging through words very often in the abstract. It is a little like the old parlour game: *What kind of a tree is he? What kind of a book, what kind of a dog?* Image by analogy, or poetry, may be the only way we can go until medical science finds a way to bridge your eyes over to my brain and your ears over to mine. We both have to get out of our in-between positions. Only in direct transmission will truth be found, and it may very well prove to be startling.

Now we must conclude that all of this is as true for cats as it is for us. Unless we can demonstrate that they have some form of telepathic projection (and a lot of people say they do), why should we assume that any two cats watching a person asleep on a couch see the same thing or experience the same emotion or whatever is the appropriate word for what cats feel? ("Emotion" is probably not a perfect choice.) They can't, of course, and intelligent as cats are, they are probably as subjective as any other species capable of some degree of cognition. There is, then, a problem. Cats can't deal with analogies, or at least we may assume that to be true. No poems, no spoken or implied *likes* or *as ifs*, just the facts, and each cat like each of us has its own facts that it must deal with. If all of this seems to place each living creature on an island of its own trying to cross over to others of its own kind, and perhaps to other kinds of sentient beings as well to explain what the realities are, that is probably just the way it is here on earth.

The cat we have been talking about in this effort is a bundle of interpreted generalisations just as books about people are. We have to live with that not only here but in all of our communications. Cats and people are keepers of secrets, for there is no way for either species not to be.

Time and again in this book I have placed the cat and ourselves in analogous positions although I vowed to avoid that pitfall whenever I could. As it turns out, that was not possible because nothing could be quantified without some kind of comparison. Using a dog, ape, or crocodile would not have worked well in any but a very few instances because those animals, all animals, are as little understood by us as the cat is. No sense comparing apples to oranges for someone who doesn't know either fruit. The irony is that any time the man/cat comparison or analogy has been made, it has been a unique happening on the receiving

end. For someone who is colour-blind, the chapter on the cat's eyesight, I am sure, is one thing, quite different from what it would be for someone with what we like to think of as a full range of colour vision. My chapter about hearing can be read by a hearing person or a deaf person or a person in between where most of us dwell. Each person might read different things into what is being said. If you have owned cats and cared about them, you will read all of this one way. If cats are strangers to you (you probably won't be reading this book), all of this may border on the lunatic, this concern for cats and what they think if they think (they do!), what they see since they obviously see.

I have allowed a little of the far-out to creep into my considerations—things like subatomic particles and celestial music. That is appropriate in a way only true cat lovers can understand. Cats are far-out and that must be much of their appeal. Everything we find out about the world around us, from the possibility of new moons to tectonic plates and shifting continents, from sociobiology to ethology, proves to us we are always (and perhaps always will be, although that is a very long time) on the edge of the far-out. The fact that the earth revolves around the sun and not according to the Ptolemaic formula the other way, and the fact that you can't sail westward and fall off the planet, is nothing when compared to what we have found out about genetics in the last few years alone. All of our science, from space travel to organ transplants, is fresh and new every morning when we get up. It is easy to get all tangled up in the nasty little things that happen on this planet (because of our own unbelievable behaviour) and forget about the grand openings we are going through. And that is right where the cat belongs, at the gateway of the about-to-be revealed, which is perhaps why so many scientists have enjoyed its company. I have no doubt that the first companion animal in space (put aboard to relieve the tedium of long-term space travellers) will be a cat. It will probably be a Sphinx to keep hair from drifting weightlessly into the computer banks. For neophytes, Sphinx cats are bald.

There is probably not a person alive who can truly remember the first time he was aware of the cat's existence. We saw them in our picture books before we went to school and heard about them in the stories we were told. (I did, however, meet a child from a culturally deprived New York City home who was in a special school—Green Chimneys—where animals are used to help such children bridge across into the real world of their peers. At the age of ten he was brought to the school by court order and on his second day was given some rabbits to care for. The kid remembers that day very well. He had to ask one of the other kids what the rabbits were. He went on to win several awards for the rabbits he bred.) But for most of us, cats have always been there in one form or another. The next time you stroke a cat, try to remember when the first time you touched a cat might have been. Most of us can't. Cats are and always were there, even for people who came from homes without pets. Someone had a cat somewhere. They are a given.

It was probably that way for the human race and its experience with cats. There was probably no time at which people could say: "I saw a cat today. I'd heard about them. What a nice-looking animal that is.'

And there was probably no one point at which people started to breed in certain characteristics or breed others out. That is almost surely true since at the point where the cat started figuring in human history, nobody knew anything about genetics or heredity. The first steps towards producing a domestic species were serendipitous. They had to be. People kept the animals they liked, and together in captivity they bred and produced young with the likeable characteristics enhanced until those nice genes prevailed. If cats of a certain colour were lucky or good omens, they were the ones that were encouraged to breed with each other, and so the gene for that colour was passed along.

The point is, the cat crept up on us. For close to four millennia we have been moving in tandem through wars and famines and stages of ignorance, as we, at least, have been marching toward enlightenment. There were cats in Egyptian homes (not so different from our own homes since they adored their cats) and there were cats in and around homes in the Middle Ages and there are cats in and around the house where this is being written. Interestingly enough, the cats of today may be a little cooler in temperament than the cats in ancient Egypt (a little cooler, not much) but probably not a whit more intelligent. If we are to use dogs as a directly analogous species, cats would be less intelligent in our time than four thousand years ago because wolves are almost inevitably very much more intelligent than dogs. The wolf brain is half again as large as a dog's on a pound-for-pound of body weight basis. However, we don't know that that analogy does hold up. There is the distinct possibility that it does not, and besides, there is more to intelligence than gram of brain to pound of muscle, fat, and bone.

In our culture, then, and a good many that have led up to it, the cat has been one of the constants. We have done everything from ignore to worship it, from love to hate it. And through all that thick and thin the cat has been watching us and watching everything else around it. If you have more than one cat, make a note of what one cat does while the other uses the litter tray. It is likely to sit and watch, not because it is some kind of weird *voyeur* but because it is inherently interested in anything that occurs—anything that anything or anyone else does. How many hundreds of millions of people have been watched by a like number of cats for how many billions of hours I cannot imagine, but the cat has obviously not had its fill. It will still watch every chance it gets in expectation of what I cannot imagine and drawing what conclusions I would rather not say. Perhaps I don't want to know.

Most doctors today (except allergists) will tell you that we are better off for having had the cat, and that individuals bonded to a companion animal will probably have longer, generally happier and healthier lives. Cats are a tonic, they are a laugh, they are a cuddle, they are at least pretty just about all of the time and beautiful some of the time. They are demanding, and they are also giving for people who are accepting. Who cares if they want to watch? Why not, if it gives them pleasure? If I knew what they wanted, I would even perform for them. It is more than likely that I already do without even knowing it. It is little enough to offer in return for the pleasure of this very old and true relationship.

Drawing by Steinlen

PICTURE SOURCES

The estate of Harold Philip Stern
    page 131

Metropolitan Museum of Art
    pages 29, 33, 48, 52, 64, 72, 95, 127, 136, 140, 179, 181

Karin E. Sanborn
    pages 13, 66, 82, 126, 161, 171, 176

The New York Public Library Picture Collection
    pages 27, 43, 50, 89, 102, 107, 123, 134, 147, 151, 167

Paul Sachs
    pages 37, 70, 78, 87, 92, 114, 119, 156, 164

Cinders Trim (by kind permission)
    pages 2, 19, 76

Private collection
    pages 6, 23, 25, 40, 55, 58, 61, 99, 110, 139, 144

Drawing by Steinlen

INDEX